Cambridge Elements ≡

Elements in Metaphysics
edited by
Tuomas E. Tahko
University of Bristol

T0287034

CHEMISTRY'S
METAPHYSICS

Vanessa A. Seifert
National and Kapodistrian University of Athens

CAMBRIDGE
UNIVERSITY PRESS

CAMBRIDGE
UNIVERSITY PRESS

Shaftesbury Road, Cambridge CB2 8EA, United Kingdom

One Liberty Plaza, 20th Floor, New York, NY 10006, USA

477 Williamstown Road, Port Melbourne, VIC 3207, Australia

314–321, 3rd Floor, Plot 3, Splendor Forum, Jasola District Centre,
New Delhi – 110025, India

103 Penang Road, #05–06/07, Visioncrest Commercial, Singapore 238467

Cambridge University Press is part of Cambridge University Press & Assessment,
a department of the University of Cambridge.

We share the University's mission to contribute to society through the pursuit of
education, learning and research at the highest international levels of excellence.

www.cambridge.org
Information on this title: www.cambridge.org/9781009467865

DOI: 10.1017/9781009238861

© Vanessa A. Seifert 2023

This work is in copyright. It is subject to statutory exceptions and to the provisions
of relevant licensing agreements; with the exception of the Creative Commons version
the link for which is provided below, no reproduction of any part of this work may take
place without the written permission of Cambridge University Press & Assessment.

An online version of this work is published at doi.org/10.1017/9781009238861 under
a Creative Commons Open Access license CC-BY-NC-ND 4.0 which permits re-use,
distribution and reproduction in any medium for non-commercial purposes providing
appropriate credit to the original work is given. You may not distribute derivative
works without permission. To view a copy of this license, visit
https://creativecommons.org/licenses/by-nc-nd/4.0

All versions of this work may contain content reproduced under license from third
parties.

Permission to reproduce this third-party content must be obtained from these
third-parties directly.

When citing this work, please include a reference to the DOI 10.1017/9781009238861

First published 2023

A catalogue record for this publication is available from the British Library

ISBN 978-1-009-46786-5 Hardback
ISBN 978-1-009-23882-3 Paperback
ISSN 2633-9862 (online)
ISSN 2633-9854 (print)

Cambridge University Press & Assessment has no responsibility for the persistence
or accuracy of URLs for external or third-party internet websites referred to in this
publication and does not guarantee that any content on such websites is, or will
remain, accurate or appropriate.

Chemistry's Metaphysics

Elements in Metaphysics

DOI: 10.1017/9781009238861
First published online: November 2023

Vanessa A. Seifert
National and Kapodistrian University of Athens

Author for correspondence: Vanessa A. Seifert, seifertvan@phs.uoa.gr

Abstract: The place of chemistry in the metaphysics of science may be viewed as peripheral compared to physics and biology. However, a metaphysics of science that disregards chemistry would be incomplete and ill-informed. This Element establishes this claim by showing how key metaphysical issues are informed by drawing on chemistry. Five metaphysical topics are investigated: natural kinds, scientific realism, reduction, laws and causation. These topics are spelled out from the perspective of ten chemical case studies, each of which illuminates the novel ways that metaphysics of science can be informed by chemistry. This title is also available as Open Access on Cambridge Core.

Keywords: philosophy of chemistry, metaphysics of chemistry, realism and chemistry, reduction of chemistry, chemical kinds, laws in chemistry, causation in chemistry

© Vanessa A. Seifert 2023

ISBNs: 9781009467865 (HB), 9781009238823 (PB), 9781009238861 (OC)
ISSNs: 2633-9862 (online), 2633-9854 (print)

Contents

1 Introduction

The goal of metaphysics of science is to understand the world, its structure and fundamental ontological categories by studying the concepts, theories and explanations of science. The place of chemistry in the metaphysics of science may be viewed as peripheral compared to physics, which tells us about the fundamental behaviour of the non-living world, and biology, which deals with life. However, a metaphysics of science that disregards chemistry would be incomplete and ill-informed. The aim of this Element is to establish this claim by showing how key metaphysical issues are informed by drawing on chemistry.[1]

That chemistry can contribute to our metaphysical understanding of the world should not come as a surprise. The history of science offers several examples where the concepts, phenomena and practices that nowadays belong within the purview of chemistry played an important role in forming metaphysical world-views. Take for example Aristotle's worldview, which was widely accepted in the West up until the Scientific Revolution. Aristotle adopted Empedocles' hypothesis that there are four fundamental elements from which everything is made: air, earth, fire and water. He claimed that there is a *prima materia* (i.e. first matter) that causes these elements and brings everything into existence, thus formulating one of the most discussed accounts of causation in metaphysics (Aristotle 1999). Another example can be found in the Chinese ancient tradition, which similarly posited fundamental elements out of which everything is made. In this case, the focus was on identifying the 'primary substance' that brings all of them together (Ball 2021: 14–27). Both examples illustrate that basic concepts in the lexicon of modern chemistry (such as 'element' and 'substance') played an important part in spelling out metaphysical ideas. Not only that, but the empirical study of chemical phenomena (such as the burning of fire) was invoked to support metaphysical claims (Bartoš and King 2020).

Of course, the relation of chemistry to metaphysics is not the same as it was in the past. Before the Scientific Revolution, questions about the nature and transformation of matter were intertwined with those about the movement of planets, the meaning of life, the beginning of the universe, the nature of the soul and the fundamental categories of existence. All these questions were usually accounted for by a single overarching worldview which included – to today's standard's – metaphysical, scientific and religious hypotheses. Metaphysics and science were not separate fields of inquiry but formed a unified endeavour to understand the world and our place in it.

---

[1] Given this Element's scope, such an analysis is bound to be incomplete, leaving out other metaphysical issues that can be benefited by investigating them from a chemical perspective.

Alchemy is a paradigmatic example of how intertwined metaphysics and chemistry once were. Paracelsus – one of the most famous alchemists of the sixteenth century – proposed an alchemical philosophy that amounted to a sort of 'Theory of Everything', extending well beyond the investigation of chemical phenomena for merely practical purposes. Among other things, his alchemical theory accounted for the beginning of the universe, postulated correspondence relations between elements and planets and explained the nature of living beings in terms of chemical transformations (Ball 2021: 52–3).

Today, chemistry and metaphysics form distinct fields of study with specific domains and methods of inquiry.[2] On the one hand, chemistry is a well-defined empirical science which examines hypotheses on the constitution and transformation of matter. On the other hand, metaphysics has cast out mystical considerations that were associated with it in the past. When the focus is on science, metaphysics nowadays does not question the validity of scientific hypotheses but investigates their implications for our understanding of the world.[3]

In this context, some metaphysical questions about chemistry are:

1. Do chemical concepts – such as 'substance' and 'element' – correspond to natural kinds?
2. Do chemical bonds exist, and what is their precise nature?
3. Are atoms, molecules and their chemical properties just the result of quantum physical entities and their interactions?
4. Does the periodic table represent laws of nature?
5. Do chemical reactions express causal relations?

Some of these questions have been examined in current metaphysics more than others. Questions about realism, natural kinds and reduction have received considerable attention, whereas laws and causation in chemistry have been largely ignored.

Note that these questions may suggest a pre-established outlook to metaphysics and the acceptance of specific metaphysical principles (such as that natural kinds exist; that there are laws of nature; that there are distinct levels of reality; or that causation is a meaningful concept). Evidently, these are far from obvious, and it is not my intention to establish such presuppositions. In fact, certain chemical case studies reveal that we should perhaps revise how certain metaphysical notions are traditionally conceived (for example, see the discussion of

---

[2] Nevertheless, some might still argue that (good) metaphysics and science are part of the same endeavour.

[3] I am only referring to the metaphysics of science and not to the metaphysics which is concerned with ideas such as identity, change and persistence.

chemical kinds in Section 2). So, this Element is not merely an exercise that applies chemical case studies to pre-established metaphysical ideas. On the other hand, I do not purport to offer a novel outlook on our metaphysical understanding of the world through the study of chemistry. After all, there are practical limits to how extensively an Element like this can pursue a revisionist analysis of so many topics at once (and this is far from done here). Instead, the aim is to show how both chemistry and metaphysics can be informed by a fruitful exchange of ideas.

Such an exchange is already in place, so the discussion is framed here in the context of what has already been said in metaphysics in relation to chemistry. The choice of this starting point does not imply that the metaphysical frame-work in which such work is developed should be beyond scrutiny. While this Element does not establish new metaphysical frameworks, it is my hope that it encourages the interchange of metaphysics with chemistry, for the further development of (both revisionist and non-revisionist) metaphysics of chemistry.

The Element has three sections. Section 1 discusses natural kinds. It presents the chemical entities that are considered as candidates for natural kinds and spells out the main arguments in favour and against them being viewed as natural kinds. Four case studies are considered: elements, compounds, acids and macromolecules. Section 2 discusses realism and reduction. It presents the arguments in favour and against the reality of chemical entities and examines how their ontological status is affected by how they relate to their physical parts. Atoms and molecules, phlogiston, molecular structure and the chemical bond are examined. Section 3 investigates laws and causation from the perspective of the periodic table and chemical reactions.

2 Natural Kinds

Elements, Compounds, Acids and Macromolecules

It is very common to group things together to organise them. We identify individual objects as chairs and tables, whales and dolphins, oxygen and hydrogen and so on. Grouping things is extremely useful in everyday life and in science too, including chemistry. Take, for instance, lithium. Lithium is identified as a chemical element with a high tendency to react; that forms ionic bonds; and, when in bulk, is soft and shiny. Grouping materials as instances of lithium explains why they exhibit the chemical and physical properties they do. Interestingly, lithium itself is grouped with other elements. Chemists discovered that some of lithium's properties are not unique; similar properties are exhibited by things made of sodium, potassium, rubidium, cae-sium and francium. So, they classified these elements as alkali metals. They are now grouped together because of one common characteristic: their outermost electron occupies the s-orbital.

Categorisations highlight the similarities between the members of a group, and the dissimilarities to members of other groups. More importantly, they are crucial for the prediction and explanation of phenomena. The interactions between different chunks of matter and their individual observable properties are explained not by specifying the characteristics of each chunk, but by the fact that they are instances of a kind of matter which possesses certain unique features.

All this prompts questions that are of interest to philosophers and that can be distinguished into three broad categories (Bursten 2016: 4). First are the methodological questions. These focus on the use and value of grouping things together in scientific practice. Second are the semantic questions. These concern the semantics of natural kind terms and questions such as how the reference of kind terms is fixed determinately and correctly (if either). Third are the metaphysical questions.[4] The basic issue concerns whether the groupings we posit – especially in science – reflect 'the structure of the natural world rather than the interests and actions of human beings' (Bird and Tobin 2022).[5]

This latter issue is referred to in metaphysics as the question of natural kinds.[6] Namely, does science – through its taxonomic schemes and postulation of kinds – 'carve nature at its joints'?[7] If so, what is it that qualifies things as members of a natural kind? For example, what is it for one chunk of matter to be an instance of water and not of ammonia?

The question of natural kinds in chemistry – that is, are chemical kinds natural kinds? – takes particular form when applied to entities postulated by chemistry. For example, chemical elements are central in understanding natural kinds, representing a paradigmatic case for discussion of this topic in general (e.g. Bird 2018; Kripke 1972). Other candidate chemical kinds are compounds, mixtures, chemical bonds, acids and macromolecules (e.g. Bartol 2016; Chang 2012a; Havstad 2018; Hendry 2006a; Needham 2000; Slater 2009; Tahko 2020; Tobin 2010b). To say that any of these chemical kinds corresponds to a natural

---

[4] One could add that there are epistemological questions about natural kinds, regarding how we know and justify positing groupings in science.

[5] These three categories are interconnected, making it difficult to discuss one of them without mention of the others. The primary focus here is on the metaphysical questions, acknowledging that this inevitably results in a partial analysis of natural kinds.

[6] There is a massive literature that one could reference in relation to this topic. Given the scope of this Element, I direct the reader to the encyclopedic entry of Bird and Tobin 2022.

[7] This phrase is a translation from Plato, who was one of the first philosophers to discuss the issue (Plato 1952).

kind is to say that these groupings reflect some part of the structure of the world (see Section 3).

Section 2.1 examines which properties unify members of a chemical kind. The received view is presented – microstructural essentialism – which is applied to the case of chemical elements and compounds. Section 2.2 investigates whether chemical kinds correspond to natural or artificial kinds and presents three problems to the view that chemical kinds are natural. The case of acids is discussed. Section 2.3 examines issues about kindhood that arise when considering the interface between chemistry and biology. The case study is macromolecules.

2.1 Searching for a Unifying Property

Most debates about natural kinds in the philosophy of chemistry revolve around correctly identifying the properties which unify members of a chemical kind, with the received view being microstructural essentialism. This view states that membership in a chemical kind is conferred by its members' microstructural properties. Microstructural essentialism is often regarded as a consequence of Kripke's (1972) and Putnam's (1975) semantic analysis of kinds and their defence of semantic externalism.[8] In the philosophy of chemistry, microstructural essentialism has been defended for chemical elements and compounds by, for example, Ellis (2001), Harré (2005), Havstad (2018), Hendry (2006a) and Hoefer and Martí (2019), and has received criticism with respect to chemical elements by, for example, Bursten (2016), and to chemical compounds by, for example, Needham (2011), van Brakel (1986) and Weisberg (2006).[9] First, I discuss chemical elements.

Case I. Chemical Elements

The idea of elements existed for millennia but it is safe to say that Lavoisier gave the first rigorous definition of them. He proposed that elements are things that cannot be further decomposed by means of chemical analysis. Dalton postulated that elements are composed of 'qualitatively identical atoms', to which Mendeleev added that the property which all atoms of an element share is their atomic weight (Hendry 2005: 32).[10] In the 1920s, it was discovered that

---

[8] Semantic views are connected to metaphysical questions about natural kinds. Given the scope of this section, discussion of semantic issues is kept to a minimum. The next section revisits semantic issues to the extent that they inform the analysis of scientific realism.

[9] Given the importance of chemical examples in the general discussion about natural kinds, there are many works from the literature which I do not mention. I prioritise reference to works that focus on chemical cases.

[10] Atomic weight is the 'ratio of the average mass of the atom to the unified atomic mass unit' (IUPAC 2014: 1280).

elements can contain atoms of different atomic weights (i.e. isotopes). Given this, the International Union for Pure and Applied Chemistry (IUPAC) defined them to be distinguished by their atomic number; that is, the 'number of protons in the atomic nucleus' (IUPAC 2014: 123).[11]

Microstructural essentialism about chemical elements involves two claims. First, the property which identifies a kind-element is microstructural: it is a property that concerns the microstructure of atoms. Most proponents take this to be IUPAC's defining property of elements: atomic number (e.g. Hendry 2006a; Putnam 1975). Second, the microstructural property is essential to its kindhood. What is meant by 'essential' diverges in the literature, but one could contend that there are (at least) two interpretations.[12] First, 'essential' confers the idea that it is necessary for members of a kind to possess that property: if they do not possess it, they are not members of that kind.[13] For example, if a sample does not consist of atoms with atomic number 79, it does not qualify as an instance of gold even if it exhibits all other properties that are standardly associated with gold (such as colour and texture) (Hendry 2005: 33). The second interpretation takes a property to be essential in that it is necessary and sufficient for members of a kind (e.g. Häggqvist 2022: 32). On this view, a sample consisting of atoms with atomic number 79 is an instance of gold even if it does not exhibit the properties that one generally expects of gold (such as being shiny or malleable).

A different account of microstructural essentialism for elements is formulated by Harré (2005), who bases his account on Locke's distinction between nominal and real essences. Harré takes nominal essences to refer to a set of properties that have been selected by the scientific community at a specific historical period to pick out members of a kind. He views them as practical criteria to identify members of a kind. Real essences are the necessary and sufficient criteria for an instance to be member of a kind. Real essences are often unobservable properties and are conferred by theoretical hypotheses that are

---

[11] 'Element' refers to both 'a species of atoms' and a 'pure chemical substance composed of atoms with the same number of protons' (IUPAC 2014: 258). So the term 'element' refers to two different things: a kind of (single) atom which is uniquely identified by its atomic number, and a collection of atoms, all of which have the same atomic number. A chemical substance is '(m)atter of constant composition best characterised by the entities (molecules, formula units, atoms) it is composed of' (IUPAC 2014: 265).

[12] I thank the anonymous reviewers for drawing my attention to this distinction in the literature. See also, for example, Tobin 2010b for a detailed analysis of the different interpretations of microstructural essentialism more generally.

[13] Some philosophers argue that 'essential' cannot be analysed in terms of necessity but rather the reverse: necessity is analysed in terms of essence (e.g. Fine 1994; Lowe 2006; Tahko 2018). Also, one can talk about essences and necessity in terms of (among other things) modality, possible worlds and dispositions (Fine 1994; Lowe 2006; Tahko 2018). Given that in the philosophy of chemistry these issues are not discussed, they are disregarded.

empirically confirmable and thus revisable. In the case of elements, Harré argues that atomic number 'is meant to express an aspect of the real essences of elementary substances' (2005: 19).

Objections are raised against microstructural essentialism when applied to chemical elements.[14] These objections are (implicitly at least) addressed against the second interpretation of microstructural essentialism as they point out chemical examples in which atomic number is insufficient for correctly identifying members of an element-kind. First, take isotopes. Isotopes are '(n)uclides having the same atomic number but different mass numbers' (IUPAC 2014: 794). This means that while all members of an element possess the same number of protons in their nucleus, they can possess different numbers of neutrons. For example, the element hydrogen can be found in stable form with either zero, one or two neutrons. These three cases correspond to distinct isotopes of hydrogen: protium, deuterium and tritium, respectively.[15] Given this, it can be argued that atomic number does not distinguish correctly between kinds because, based on this property, members of the same element-kind exhibit differences in their chemical and physical behaviour. This leads to the following dilemma: we either admit that members of the same element-kind exhibit different observable properties or we deny that atomic number is sufficient to correctly pick out members of a kind.

In response to this, Hendry claims that chemists rightly do not distinguish isotopes as different kinds (2006a: 868). Indeed, protium, deuterium and tritium are regarded as instances of the same element (hydrogen), occupying a single space in the periodic table. This is empirically justified because while hydrogen exhibits chemical and physical differences in its three isotopic forms (including in some instances, in its toxicity, boiling point, density and reactivity), most differentiations in mass numbers have negligible observable differences. As Hendry states, 'the isotope effect in hydrogen is an extreme case: a monster, not a paradigm' (2006a: 868).

However, Bursten points out that there are also other properties (apart from isotopy) that lead to observable differences among members of an element-kind. These concern the size, shape and dimensionality of the collection of atoms that makes up a pure substance (Bursten 2016: 14). For example, a collection of 100 gold atoms (suspended in a prepared solution) exhibits different properties from a collection of a billion gold atoms (Bursten 2016: 1). The texture and appearance of the two collections differ: the lump of a billion gold atoms is shiny and yellow, but the hundred gold atoms in a solution are red or black (Bursten 2016: 2). Moreover, at the nanoscale, differences in size, shape and surface lead to

---

[14] Objections that are important to the critique of microstructural essentialism but require the extensive analysis of semantic and methodological issues are not discussed (e.g. LaPorte 1996).

[15] In the scientific literature, the term 'hydrogen' sometimes refers only to protium.

differences in the material's physical properties (such as conductivity and ductil-
ity), and to differences in chemical properties (including chemical reactivity).
According to Bursten, this is a problem for microstructural essentialism because
'(a)ll this is to say that the macroscopic kindhood of my collection of gold atoms
is underdetermined by solely specifying the identity of the atoms involved'
(2016: 2). So, one is faced with a similar dilemma as in the case of isotopes:
either accept that an element-kind exhibits different macroscopic properties
depending on the size, shape and surface of the corresponding collection of
atoms or deny that atomic number is sufficient to differentiate between observ-
ably distinct kinds of matter (Bursten 2016: 2).

   In light of this, Bursten proposes reactivity as the correct property to pick out
members of a kind.[16] As she states, 'fundamental chemical kinds should be
individuated such that no two kinds enter into all the same chemical reactions
and no two members of one kind enter into different reactions' (2014: 639).
Interestingly, despite dismissing microstructure as essential to chemical kinds,
she retains its importance in the sense that it explains the reactivity of chemical
kinds. She claims that microstructure and reactivity form an asymmetric relationship: microstructure grounds, justifies and explains the reactivity of a kind
(and not vice versa) (Bursten 2014: 644).

   Note also that for Bursten microstructure should not be understood as referring solely to the atomic number of an element, but to a richer set of microstructural information (2014: 639). She distinguishes between two types of so-called
Chemical Microstructural Properties (CMPs): monadic and relational CMPs.[17]
Monadic CMPs concern the individual properties of atoms and include, apart
from atomic number, the number of neutrons (and thus isotopic information) as
well as electronic structure. Relational CMPs include properties concerning the
relations among atoms, such as the ratio of species of atoms in a molecule and
the geometric properties of molecules. Both proposed revisions offer a more
complete account of what microstructure involves. As such, one could wonder
why this amended understanding of microstructure does not resolve Bursten's
objection to microstructural essentialism. After all, if these properties are
included in our understanding of microstructure, can we not argue that this
enriched notion is sufficient to being member of an element-kind?[18] We return
to this in the discussion of chemical compounds.

---

[16] Bursten's proposal is not primarily metaphysical as she is not concerned with the essence of
chemical kinds. Also, her proposal applies to chemical elements and chemical compounds.
[17] While Bursten does not formulate this distinction in terms of intrinsic versus extrinsic properties,
it is plausible that it could be cast in these terms.
[18] An alternative response to Bursten is to claim that microstructure determines a range of disposi-
tional properties that become manifest only under certain conditions (including conditions of size
and scale).

Case II. Chemical Compounds

While IUPAC does not offer a definition of compounds, compounds are stand-ardly understood as collections of identical molecular entities. Similarly to element-kinds, microstructural essentialism for compound-kinds takes that a chunk of matter is member of a compound-kind in virtue of its microstructural properties. For example, a jug of liquid is member of the kind-water because of its microstructure; namely, it consists of H_2O molecules. This idea is often conferred in the literature by the phrase 'Water is H_2O' or 'Water = H_2O' and has prompted extensive criticisms. While I do not restrict my analysis of this view to either of the two interpretations of 'essential' presented at the beginning of this section, it is interesting to note that insofar as '=' is understood as a symmetric identity relation, statements of the form 'Water = H_2O' may be understood as taking H_2O to be both necessary and sufficient to being water.[19]

This reading is further reinforced by the fact that most objections seem to (implicitly) address (again) the second interpretation of 'essential'. First, take the problem of isotopes, which carries over to the case of compounds. Isotopes form distinct isotopic compounds (also called isotopic isomers; Weisberg 2006). For example, there are three isotopes for hydrogen and three for oxygen, resulting in different combinations between them that produce different isotopic variants for water. The problem with this is not that substances with distinct isotopic properties are all members of the same compound-kind (i.e. the kind-water). This is to be expected from a microstructural essentialist perspective as the latter regards distinct isotopes to be members of the same element-kind. Instead, the problem with isotopic compounds is that certain combinations of isotopes lead to different macroscopic properties that are not standardly associ-ated with the compound-kind of which they are members. For example, con-sider a substance consisting mainly of deuterium oxide, D_2O (called heavy water). This is an isotopic variant of H_2O and, as such, microstructural essen-tialists regard it a member of the kind-water. However, this compound is highly toxic and undrinkable. Therefore, it exhibits an important observable diver-gence from the properties usually associated with water (Hendry 2012a: 62–3). So, the dilemma is similar to that previously raised about element-kinds: we either admit that members of the same compound-kind exhibit different observ-able properties (due to their isotopic variance) or we deny that being H_2O is sufficient to being water.

Despite this, Hendry maintains that 'being H_2O is the only chemical require-ment that is relevant to being water; it is the only requirement of any kind that is necessary to being water' (2012a: 63). As with the case of isotopes, he points

---

[19] Sincere thanks to the anonymous reviewer who pointed this out.

out that water is mostly found as a drinkable non-toxic substance and the microstructural properties which describe its elemental composition success-fully explain the standard properties associated with water. This view is more generally based on what he calls the 'core conception' of a chemical element, which consists of three assumptions: (a) elements survive chemical change; (b) compounds are composed of elements; and (c) the elemental composition of compounds explains their behaviour (Hendry 2006b). On this view, if we accept these assumptions, then we can maintain microstructural essentialism about chemical compounds.[20]

However, apart from isotopic compounds, there are also isomers which seem to reinforce the problem for microstructural essentialism. An isomer is '(o)ne of several species (or molecular entities) that have the same atomic composition ... but different line formulae or different stereochemical formulae and hence different physical and/or chemical properties' (IUPAC 2014: 784). Consider ethanol and methoxymethane (Hendry 2006a: 869). Both compounds consist of the same type and number of atoms: two carbon atoms, six hydrogen atoms and one oxygen atom. However, the atoms in each case are bonded differently, resulting in the line formulae CH_3CH_2OH and CH_3OCH_3, respectively. Isomers are problematic for the microstructural essentialist because they show that elem-ental composition fails to distinguish between compounds that not only have different physical and chemical properties but also – more importantly – are regarded by scientists as distinct kinds of compounds.

This problem can be resolved if 'microstructural properties' include not just information about the elemental composition of compounds but also structural information about atomic connectivity and molecular structure (e.g. McFarland 2018; this is also similar to adopting Bursten's notion of relational CMPs). After all, structure is a collective term which includes all properties that specify the spatial arrangement of the atoms that constitute a molecule, such as the number and types of chemical bonds, bond length, bond angles and so on. By enriching the notion of microstructural properties, one can retain the thesis that the essence of compound-kinds (including isomers) is conferred by their microstructure.

A third problem for the microstructural essentialist arises with mixtures, as the specification of microstructure does not seem to suffice to distinguish mixtures from compounds. A mixture is a 'portion of matter consisting of two or more chemical substances' (IUPAC 2014: 941). According to Needham, a microstructural essentialist cannot distinguish between – say – water and a homogeneous mixture of hydrogen and oxygen that has the same elemental

---

[20] I am not certain if Hendry's proposal concerns microstructural essentialism as per the first, second or both interpretations of 'essential', so I leave this open.

proportions as water (2011: 11). This is because both samples have the same elemental composition and in practice scientists distinguish them by specifying their macroscopic differences, such as their melting points and reactivities (Needham 2011: 11–12). One plausible reply to this is that Needham's point expresses an epistemic (and perhaps semantic) difficulty in identifying compound-kinds. From a metaphysical perspective, a mixture of hydrogen and oxygen is distinct from water in terms of its microstructure, regardless of whether in practice we invoke macroscopic properties to differentiate between them.

A more pressing worry is that microstructural essentialism does not conform to our best scientific understanding of the chemical world. As Needham (2011) and Häggqvist (2022: 32) point out, the physical and chemical properties of compounds are influenced by factors other than their elemental composition or even structural properties. The thermodynamic conditions under which a substance is placed and its phase (i.e. solid, liquid or gas) make a difference to its observable properties (such as boiling point and density), but also to its microstructure. Consider water. In its solid phase, its microstructure is different from that in its liquid or gaseous phase. Bond lengths and angles differ, and the way H_2O molecules dynamically interact with each other in each instance (transforming back and forth into ions of H_3O^+ and OH^-) is different, with variations in the concentration of ions depending on the thermodynamic conditions of the sample (Needham 2011: 9). This suggests that there is no '*the* microstructure of water' (as Needham puts it), but variations of microstructures depending on the macroscopic conditions in which the sample is found.

A last challenge for microstructural essentialism is that resorting to microstructural properties is not even necessary to being member of a compound-kind (Needham 2011: 8–9). If this is correct, then one could argue that microstructural properties are not essential to chemical kindhood, under either of the two readings of 'essential' property (i.e. as necessary, or as necessary and sufficient). Specifically, Needham (2011) claims that one can distinguish between members of different chemical kinds by invoking solely macroscopic properties. Thermodynamics offers both theoretical grounds and specific criteria for distinguishing between chemical compounds (whether in pure substances or in mixtures). For example, the unique triple point of chemical substances theoretically distinguishes between distinct isolated chemical substances.[21] Moreover, the Gibbs phase rule offers criteria to distinguish between chemical substances in a mixture (Needham 2011: 8).

---

[21] The triple point of a substance refers to the temperature and pressure at which its liquid, solid and gaseous phases are in equilibrium.

However, dismissing microstructure as being necessary to chemical kinds overlooks an important idea about microstructure; namely, that it has some form of metaphysical priority (e.g. Goodwin 2011; Tobin 2010b). Put differently, one cannot dismiss that the elemental constitution of a compound is what largely explains (if not somehow determines) its resulting behaviour (Häggqvist 2022: 32; Hoefer and Martí 2019: 12). Hendry makes a similar point when he states that H_2O molecules should be seen as the 'ingredients' in water that need not persist yet are essential in forming the compound water (2006a: 872). So, dismissing microstructure as necessary to the identification of a chemical kind distorts an important fact about the role of microstructure in chemistry.

Overall, what sort of property correctly distinguishes between chemical kinds and whether (and in what way) there is an essential property to them have been one of the most debated questions in philosophy of chemistry. This debate is ongoing and there are regularly new responses. The next section moves to a connected yet distinct question about chemical kinds: do they correspond to natural kinds, or do they represent artificial groupings?

2.2 Natural or Artificial?

There is a lot of discussion about what renders a grouping a natural kind, and various criteria have been proposed for that purpose (e.g. Tahko 2021: ch.4 for an overview). These criteria include for members of a kind to possess a common property (that may also need to be a natural property); the ability to formulate successful inductive generalisations; that kinds are somehow distinct from each other; that their members are not subsumed into other kinds; and so on. I do not examine all the criteria that have been offered, nor discuss which of them are necessary or sufficient for natural kindhood (if any). The debate is ongoing, so much so that the very distinction between natural and artificial kinds is put into question (e.g. Franklin-Hall 2015; Magnus 2018). For present purposes, I sketch some of the requirements that are more or less accepted to apply to natural kinds, and with regard to which there are interesting points to flesh out from the perspective of chemistry. From this it is shown that the discussion of chemical kinds as candidate natural kinds requires not just an extensive analysis of the scientific details pertaining to those groupings but also potentially a revision of how we understand natural kinds more broadly.

In general, we have good reasons to think that chemical classifications correspond to natural kinds. First, chemical classifications allow the formulation of empirically successful inductive generalisations (e.g. Mill 1884; Quine 1969; Whewell 1860). Induction is the cornerstone of modern science. Scientists carefully examine the world with the aim of proposing generalised descriptions that apply – under specified sets of conditions – to a range of phenomena. For example, by studying samples of copper, silver and gold, chemists infer that every and all instances of the kind-metal (in the past, present and future) are conductors of electricity (given a well-defined set of conditions).[22]

This in turn brings us to the explanatory and predictive power associated with natural kinds. It is in virtue of belonging to a kind that chemists explain and predict how particular instances of matter behave. For example, that copper wires conduct electricity is explained by the generalisation that all metals conduct electricity. This in turn is explained by recourse to the common properties the members of the kind-metal share. Metals contain free electrons in the outer shell of their atoms, meaning that these electrons are not associated with a specific atom nor form part of a specific chemical bond, thus allowing them to move freely and resulting in the production of an electric current. This explanation applies to all members of the kind-metal and allows us to understand why each and every instance of that kind exhibits electrical behaviour.

But there are other requirements for natural kindhood that seem to fail with respect to chemical classifications. First is the requirement that all members of a kind possess some common properties according to which they are grouped together. As we saw in the previous section, microstructural essentialism claims that members of element-kinds and compound-kinds share their microstructure. Despite disagreements on whether microstructure is essential or not (and in what manner), both microstructural essentialists and their challengers believe that there is some property that all members of these kinds share. This is not evidently so for all groupings posited in chemistry. In particular, there is a chemical case which – unlike elements and compounds – has been denied having a (set of) unique property(-ies) by which all its members are grouped together. If we accept that members of a natural kind need to share a common property, then groupings whose members do not may be regarded as artificial classifications. Such a potential case is acids.

Case III. Acids

An acid is a 'molecular entity or chemical species capable of donating a hydrogen (proton) (see Brønsted acid) or capable of forming a covalent bond with an electron pair (see Lewis acid)' (IUPAC 2014: 21). Apart from the Brønsted and

---

[22] I do not advocate that metals are natural kinds. I employ them as candidate kinds that satisfy some of the requirements for natural kindhood. Whether they are indeed natural kinds has to be investigated separately. My suspicion is that if one maintains the 'hierarchy requirement' for kindhood, then they cannot be admitted as natural kinds because their members are subsumed into different element-kinds. However, if one drops this requirement (as per, e.g. Khalidi 1998; Tobin 2010a), then metals may maintain their status as natural kinds.

the Lewis acid, IUPAC presents additional concepts and definitions of acidity, including for hard acids, soft acids, carboxylic acids, oxoacids and sulfonic acids. According to Chang (2012a), this definitional and conceptual plurality is indicative of a 'messiness' in how acids are understood and grouped into categories. This messiness arises because there is no unique set of properties that is commonly shared by acids *simpliciter*. Instead, there is a multiplicity of distinct and incommensurable concepts associated with the term 'acid'. Acidity lacks a uniform definition that applies to all recognised instances of acids, but more importantly 'a unified theory' that explains their behaviour (Chang 2012a: 697). The only reason why 'acid' is still used is due to 'the persistence of the quotidian concept' (Chang 2012a: 690). In this context, acids seem to fail a central requirement for natural kinds; namely, that all its members share a set of common properties. Therefore, acids do not correspond to a natural kind.

One can resist this claim in different ways. First, even if acids do not correspond to natural kinds, this does not imply that we cannot accept subtypes of acids as natural kinds. For example, we could argue that there are different kinds of acids, each representing a natural category (this would include the Lewis acid and the Brønsted acid as distinct kinds). This is in line with Dupré's 'promiscuous realism', which he defends for biological kinds (1993; also Hendry 2006a: 865). On this view, there is no unique privileged way of grouping things in the world. One can taxonomise objects in countless ways, all of which are natural.[23]

Alternatively, one could maintain that acids *simpliciter* correspond to a natural kind. This could be supported by accepting Scerri's objections against the empirical basis of Chang's argument. Scerri claims that the Brønsted and Lewis acids are not distinct, incommensurable concepts of acidity. This is because the Lewis definition picks out all members of the acid-kind, including those of the Brønsted acid-group (Scerri 2022: 14–15). So, the Lewis definition identifies the correct property that is shared by all instances of acids.

Another way to resist Chang's claim is by pointing out that it is not necessary that we successfully pick out the members of a kind by invoking their true common property. This is broadly based on Locke's distinction between real and nominal essences, where real essences are 'the very being of any thing, whereby it is, what it is' and nominal essences are those (observable) features that help us distinguish between substances (Locke 1689: III.iii.15).[24] According to Locke, while nominal essences follow from real essences, one

---

[23] Chang states that he follows the spirit of Dupré's position. However, it is not clear how strongly committed he is to the metaphysical aspect of natural kinds, as he also states that kinds refer 'to a classificatory concept, rather than a collection of objects' (Chang 2015b: 33).

[24] We shouldn't conflate Locke's understanding of substances with its chemical understanding.

need not know the real essences of a kind in order to pick out its members. Instead, members of a kind are usually picked through their nominal essences.

One can apply this idea to acids. Via the Lewis and Brønsted acids, scientists develop descriptions that involve reference to various observable properties which they invoke depending on the needs and uses they have. Such properties may not be suitable for picking out every and all members of the kind-acid. Nevertheless, their success to identify a subset of those members may be due to the real (yet unknown) property that unifies all instances of that kind. Therefore, the messiness of acids need not be viewed as evidence of them not being a natural kind. Instead, it could be indicative of an epistemological messiness where different descriptions pick out correctly some (not all) instances of acids.

This concludes the analysis of acids as candidate natural kinds. It revealed that identifying the unifying property of membership to a kind is not straight-forwardly satisfied by all chemical kinds. There are also other requirements that may not be met by candidate chemical kinds. The remainder of this section discusses two such criteria and shows that they are not uncontroversially met by even the most paradigmatic cases of chemical kinds.

The first is that kinds are categorically distinct (e.g. Ellis 2001). That is, there is a clear-cut distinction between kinds; there cannot be a 'smooth transition from one kind to another' (Bird and Tobin 2022). Ellis claims that chemical elements satisfy this requirement because distinct element-kinds are clearly separated by their atomic number (2002: 26). Element-kinds are distinguished by their atomic number, which is a natural number. Starting with atomic number 1 (for hydrogen), they are arranged in the periodic table in increasing atomic number. So, elements which are positioned next to each other in the periodic table have no hidden element between them.

If we accept this as a criterion for natural kindhood, then it does not apply to a paradigmatic example of chemical kinds; namely, chemical compounds. Recall that some compound-kinds only differ in terms of their structure; they are distinct isomers. In these cases, Needham (2000) and van Brakel (2000) point out that there is no clear microstructural distinction between isomers. Even if we incorporate molecular structure as part of the essence of compounds, there will always be some overlap between members of seemingly distinct (isomer) compound-kinds. This is because molecular structure is a vague con-cept: there is no clear line separating one isomeric structure from another when differentiating them in terms of quantitative differences in their bond angles, nuclear distances and so on. This reveals a general problem with compound-kinds. Structure is a dynamic property: the spatial arrangement of atoms in a molecule is continuously changing and the structures which are depicted by chemical representations are nothing more than idealised freeze motion images.

If we require for natural kinds to be distinct, as Ellis does, then this is evidence that compounds are not natural kinds.

One could reply that this is problematic only if we assume, from the microstructural essentialist perspective, that microstructure is both necessary and sufficient for kindhood. However, if we admit macroscopic properties as part of the essence of compound-kinds, then this suffices to distinguish isomer-kinds (i.e. by invoking macroscopic differences). While this seems to solve the semantic problem (of how to pick out members of a kind), it may not resolve the metaphysical issue, which is whether there exist distinct categories of isomeric structures. If structure is a vague concept then – at least when it comes to compounds that differ only in terms of their structure – there does not seem a way out of the fact that isomers are not distinct kinds.

Another requirement for natural kindhood is that the property which unifies all members of a kind is natural.[25] What we mean by 'natural' allows many interpretations and we would exhaust the length of this Element to analyse it. To avoid this, I assume that whatever 'natural property' means, it is a property whose value is not determined by the pragmatic purposes of the scientists. I explain this by means of an example. Specifically, I explicate how members of compound-kinds are unified by what we might think of as an unnatural property; namely, their stability. If this is the case, then it constitutes further evidence that compounds may not be natural kinds.

Regardless of whether we accept only microstructure as essential or take macroscopic properties as necessary to picking out members of compound-kinds, chemists always identify a compound-kind when it is thermodynamically stable. That is, they dismiss an unstable substance as a kind. However, the choice of when a substance is stable or not is a pragmatic choice, determined by the heuristic considerations of scientists. Put differently, stability – as a property of compound-kinds – is an unnatural property. This is because its value is determined by the choices of scientists.

Stability 'expresses a thermodynamic property which is quantitatively measured by relative molar standard Gibbs energies' (ΔG; IUPAC 2014: 1432). For example, 'a chemical species A is more stable than its isomer B if $\Delta_r G° > 0$ for the (real or hypothetical) reaction A -> B under standard conditions' (IUPAC 2014: 1432).[26] This shows that a chemical species is stable with respect to

---

[25] This requirement is contested because (among other reasons) some do not accept the distinction between natural kinds and properties (e.g. Tobin 2013). Tahko (2022) also argues that searching for a property that unifies members of a kind breaks down for paradigmatic cases of kinds (namely, electrons), rendering it an unsuitable requirement for natural kindhood.

[26] 'Chemical compound' is not included in the glossary of IUPAC 2014, but it is safe to assume that it is equivalent to 'chemical species'.

'some explicitly stated or implicitly assumed standard' (IUPAC 2014: 1432). The standard is set by convention and usually to the thermodynamic values that are 'characterized by a standard pressure, molality or amount concentration' (IUPAC 2014: 1438).

So, whether a compound is stable depends on a thermodynamic property (i.e. the Gibbs energy, G), whose value is determined by the specific thermodynamic conditions in which we consider that compound. The problem with this is that there is no principled reason why a given set of thermodynamic conditions should be selected where some compound is stable whereas another is not. Under different conditions, the reverse is plausible: the formerly stable compound is unstable, and the latter is stable. Why should we pick one set of conditions over another? Couldn't we consider – say – ions of NH_3 (such as ammonium NH^+_4) as compound-kinds if there are some conditions in which they are stable?

Could we dispense of stability if we invoke a different property to unify members of compound-kinds, such as Bursten's proposal of reactivity? The same problem arises. IUPAC's definition of reactivity is this: 'A species is said to be more reactive or to have a higher reactivity in some given context than some other (reference) species if it has a larger rate constant for a specified elementary reaction. *The term has meaning only by reference to some explicitly stated or implicitly assumed set of conditions*' (2014: 1261).[27] This suggests that whether a compound is reactive is determined by the conditions in which it is considered: under some conditions it is more reactive than another compound, and under different conditions it is less. Which thermodynamic conditions we consider as standard is a pragmatic choice. More importantly, there does not seem to be any principled metaphysical priority of one set of conditions over another.

Could a similar worry be expressed about element-kinds? No. Elements are not standardly identified as stable entities; far from it.[28] Many elements in the periodic table are highly unstable under standard conditions. The admittance of radioactive elements (i.e. elements which undergo spontaneous nuclear transformations) is an illuminating evidence of this. Certain radioactive elements, such as francium, are so rare that there are only 30 g found on earth's crust. Oganesson, with atomic number 118, does not naturally occur on earth and has

---

[27] Italics added here.

[28] The stability of elements should not be confused with the stability of chemical compounds. In the former case it is associated with how prone an element is to undergo a spontaneous nuclear transformation (i.e. a change in its number of protons or neutrons). In the case of compounds, stability is associated with how prone a substance is to undergo chemical transformation; that is, transform into another molecular entity(-ies).

a half-life of 1.8 milliseconds! So, whether and under what conditions elements are considered stable does not determine their admittance as element-kinds. Therefore, at least with respect to the requirement for *natural* properties, element-kinds are not threatened by a similar worry to that about compound-kinds.

These points far from settle whether elements and compounds fulfil the requirements for natural kinds. Even if the challenges I present are correct, there are probably ways in which one could maintain their natural kindhood. What these ways are is left for another occasion. In any case, an important conclusion is drawn from this analysis. Despite the extensive discussion about chemical kinds, there is still a lot to be said to convincingly claim that a chemical classification corresponds to a natural kind. One needs to look at the exact requirements for natural kindhood and examine whether they correctly apply to each chemical case. It might turn out that even the most paradigmatic cases of chemical kinds do not correspond to natural categories. Or, we might have to review how we think of the natural/artificial distinction between kinds.

2.3 Functional Kinds

As a final talking point, this section briefly discusses the role of functions in determining membership to a kind. This brings forward an interesting aspect of chemical kindhood, namely, its connection to biology and biological classification.

Case IV. Macromolecules

Certain chemical compounds are identified as kinds not in terms of their micro-structure, but in terms of a function they serve. That function may be chemical or biological. When chemical, a function is typically conferred to organic compounds by so-called functional groups, that is, 'an atom, or a group of atoms that has similar chemical properties whenever it occurs in different compounds' (IUPAC 2014: 605). Examples of functionally defined compound-kinds include alcohols, carboxylic acids, amines and ketones. When biological, a function is typically conferred to macromolecules (though not exclusively) that figure in physiological processes and is said to serve evolutionary or etiological considerations (Tahko 2020: 800).[29] Examples include proteins, genes and vitamins, and are often called biochemical kinds. Such groupings are invoked to describe biological behaviour and figure in inductive generalisations and explanations of biological phenomena.

---

[29] Macromolecules are molecules 'of high relative molecular mass, the structure of which essentially comprises the multiple repetition of units derived, actually or conceptually, from molecules of low relative molecular mass' (IUPAC 2014: 870).

The problem with functionally defined compound-kinds is that (at least part of) their unifying property is their function, undermining microstructural essentialism.[30] Tahko spells out this problem in terms of 'multiple realisation' and 'multiple determination'. Multiple realisation occurs when '(t)here may be a difference between (entities) A and B which explains why, even though each is capable of performing a certain function, they each do so in a different way' (2020: 814). For example, 'haemoglobin' refers to a group of macromolecules with different microstructures whose members are unified by their shared 'ability to bind and release oxygen' in an organism (Tahko 2020: 808). Such examples of multiple realisation putatively show that microstructure is not necessary for compounds to belong to a kind (thus undermining both interpretations of 'essential'; see Section 2.1).

Multiple determinability occurs when a microstructure realises multiple (biological or chemical) functions. An example is moonlighting proteins which have one primary structure (i.e. they are formed of the same sequence of amino acids) but fold up in different ways, thus resulting in different three-dimensional structures, each identified as a distinct kind (Tahko 2020: 804; Tobin 2010b). This is considered problematic for microstructural essentialism because (primary) microstructure is not the unifying property of protein-kinds. In fact, Tobin argues that moonlighting proteins are additionally problematic because they are 'intrinsically unstructured' or disordered, thus undermining the essential role of structure in conferring them as members of a protein-kind (2010b: 41).

There are also organic molecules that exhibit multiple determinability: an organic molecule can have a specific structure yet be considered a member of multiple chemical kinds depending on the chemical function it serves. For example, some compounds are classified as both alcohols and carboxylic acids (or, as both amines or amides). So, a compound's membership to a kind can be conferred by different chemical functions and not by its microstructure, thus undermining microstructural essentialism for chemical compounds (Goodwin 2011).

Several responses have been offered to these challenges. First, one could argue that this is evidence of some form of pluralism about natural kinds, such as Dupré's promiscuous realism (see Case III) or Slater's macromolecular pluralism. Slater (2009) claims that there is no principled way to invoke structure to distinguish between proteins; instead, there is a plurality of equally legitimate biochemical classifications. Bartol (2016) defends a 'dual theory about kinds' (see also Longy 2018). This theory purports that there are two distinct kinds of kinds: the chemical kind and the biological kind (and no biochemical kind).

---

[30] Specifying the function of a kind may be viewed as necessary or sufficient to picking members of a kind.

In this context, multiple determination putatively shows that a member of a chemical kind can contain multiple members of biological kinds. Multiple realisation shows that a member of a biological kind can contain multiple members of chemical kinds (Bartol 2016: 549). In contrast to this theory, Bellazzi (2022) argues that we should think of such groupings as genuinely biochemical kinds; that is, kinds whose membership is conferred by their microstructure and by their function.

Lastly, there are ways to defend microstructural essentialism too. Goodwin (2011) for example argues for the 'fundamental role' of structure. Based on an analysis of organic chemistry, he claims that molecular structure is fundamental because it explains why a functional group classification is appropriate at a particular instance, and because a compound's modal capacity to function a certain way is in virtue of its structure (Goodwin 2011: 538–40). (This is similar to favouring a sort of dispositionalist view about kinds.) Alternatively, one could adopt the 'powers-based subset strategy', which takes the causal powers of a (biological or chemical) function to be the proper subset of the powers of the microstructure of the compound that has that function (Tahko 2020: 806). This way, microstructural essentialism is not undermined by multiple realisability or multiple determinability because microstructure is (in the sense specified by Tahko) ontologically prior to the relevant function (Tahko 2020: 822).

Overall, whether chemical kinds are natural can only be answered on a case-by-case basis. It is likely that different chemical case studies warrant different answers as to whether they correspond to natural groupings in the world, with some representing natural kinds and others not. Moreover, as the example of chemical compounds showed, even the most paradigmatic chemical case studies for natural kinds are not definitively settled. Furthermore, this analysis may also prompt a revisionist attitude towards the very notion of natural kinds and its distinction from artificial kinds. Which route to select is left for the reader to choose!

3 Realism and Reduction

Atoms, Phlogiston, Molecular Structure and Chemical Bonds

Looking for chemical kinds is one way chemistry can be used to understand the world and its structure. One can also raise a more general question about chemistry. Namely, what is real? Do the entities, properties, processes and so on posited by chemistry exist, and are they objective and independent of chemists?[31] To what extent should we accept that what chemistry tells us about the world is true? These questions are part of the scientific realism debate.

---

[31] Unless otherwise stated, 'entities' refers to objects, properties, processes and anything else that can exist.

Scientific realism is the idea that the entities posited by our best current science exist mind-independently in the world, and that the theories and hypotheses science formulates in terms of those entities are (at least approximately) true when taken literally (e.g. Boyd 1983; Fine 1986; Laudan 1981). According to Psillos, there are three distinct theses contained within the idea of scientific realism: semantic, metaphysical and epistemic (2005: xix). This section investigates the metaphysical thesis from the perspective of chemistry; namely, does the world have an objective structure that is (partially) captured by the entities posited by our best current chemistry?[32] That is, do chemical entities inhabit the world? In this context, scientific realism denies that unobservable entities are instruments or fictions posited to manipulate the world in useful ways. Instead, the world is made of and structured by the entities and relations posited by our best current science. The goal of this section is to investigate whether these realist claims can be convincingly supported for chemical entities (and which ones specifically).

The issue of natural kinds is closely related to the issue of scientific realism. This is because when accepting scientific groupings as natural kinds, it is common to accept those kinds as real.[33] To say, for example, that the element gold is a natural kind involves the (often implicit) claim that the kind-gold exists in a mind-independent manner. There are different ways one can spell out this claim about kinds. First, one could argue that the categories we take as referring to natural kinds are real, distinct objects (distinct even from their own instances). As such, kinds are taken to exist as some sort of abstract entity or universal.[34] This position is called strong realism about kinds (Bird and Tobin 2022). On another interpretation, natural kinds are real in the sense that they reflect divisions or structures in the world. In this context, kinds are not distinct things; they are real in the sense that they reveal some part of the structure of the world. This position is called weak realism (Bird and Tobin 2022).

Some philosophers claim that to accept natural kinds is to be a scientific realist (e.g. Psillos 2005). This is sensible when one interprets the issue of natural kinds from a weak realist perspective. In this context, scientific realism can be formulated as the idea that the 'world has a definite and mind-independent natural-kind structure' (Psillos 2005: xvii). On the other hand, for a strong realist about kinds the issue of natural kinds is not settled by

---

[32] Semantic issues around truth and how it is assigned to theoretical assertions, as well as issues regarding reference, are largely overlooked.

[33] This is not always the case. Nominalists about kinds may believe that scientific groupings are just artificial or may accept that the instances of a kind are real but not the kind itself.

[34] There are different ways one can take kinds to be an abstract entity or universal. For example, Hawley and Bird (2011) view them as complex universals and Lowe (1998) as substantial universals.

adopting scientific realism. This is because there is an additional question to answer; namely, do natural kinds exist as distinct objects in the world?[35]

Perhaps adherence to scientific realism does not require the acceptance of natural kinds either from a strong or a weak realist perspective. For example, I could believe that the air I now breathe contains oxygen or that my necklace in the drawer is made of gold, and that these things exist independently of me conceiving them but make no commitment to any groupings into which they may fall. Such a view is, for instance, proposed for certain biological kinds, as it is difficult to identify common properties shared by all their instances (e.g. Hull 1978). Another option is to be a realist about things in the world yet believe that such things are only members of artificial groupings (e.g. Chakravartty 2007). On the other hand, one might argue that it is not possible to deny the existence of natural kinds and be a scientific realist at the same time. On this view, if I believe that a chemical reaction occurs when I am breathing oxygen that leads to the production of carbon dioxide, it is because I adhere to the generalisations posited by science about those entities as categories, aka kinds.

So, there are different ways to be a realist about different things, and the realist question is far from settled even if we take as decisive the arguments presented in Section 2 in favour and against chemical kinds. In fact, Section 2 showed that there are different ways to understand natural kinds and different things one can regard as such. Inevitably, this affects the extent to which a commitment to realism in chemistry implies a commitment to chemical kindhood (and vice versa) that deserves further investigation. In any case, the only restriction imposed on any position about realism and kinds is that it is logically consistent and consistent with the results of our best current chemistry.

The relations between realism and kinds are not further investigated. Henceforth, the question of realism in chemistry is investigated separately. This is not uncommon practice. Whether chemical entities are natural kinds is usually discussed separately from the debate about their reality.

Section 3.1 presents the realist and anti-realist arguments that have been formulated with respect to chemical entities and particularly about atoms, molecules and phlogiston. Section 3.2 discusses chemistry's relation to quantum physics: it presents a central antireductionist argument and two metaphysical accounts that have been produced by its acceptance (strong emergence and ontological pluralism). The case of molecular structure is examined. Section 3.3 presents an account of unity which offers an alternative way of understanding chemistry's relation to quantum physics that maintains the reality of chemical stuff. The case study is the chemical bond.

---

[35] I do not investigate this.

3.1 Realism in Chemistry

There are three questions that are standardly addressed in discussions of realism about science, and they can all be asked about chemistry:

1. Should we be realists about unobservable chemical entities?
2. To what extent should we believe in the reality of chemical entities given that science (including chemistry) is constantly revised and amended?
3. Should we believe in the reality of chemical entities given that they are not fundamental but composed of other (physical) entities?

The first two questions are intertwined, and the rest of this section addresses them together. The next section addresses the third.

There are some things we directly observe through our senses and others that we don't. Chemistry posits both sorts of things. Substances and mixtures, like salted water or silver coins, are directly observable as they can be perceived by our senses without the use of instruments.[36] Other chemical entities cannot be observed directly, such as atoms, molecules and chemical bonds. In this case, chemists posit those entities as part of their overall theoretical set-up and claim to detect them with the use of instruments.

Interestingly, scientists often claim to 'observe' such entities too. For example, atomic force microscopy (AFM) is said to offer high-resolution images of certain atoms, molecules and their structures (Kumaki 2016). However, these images are the result of the force interactions between the tip of the AFM instrument and the examined sample. To interpret and visualise this result in the form of an image, one makes assumptions drawn from optics, electromagnetism and chemistry. Without them it would not be possible to produce the images. So even if we grant AFM as a means of observation, this sort of observation is made possible due to some accepted theoretical assumptions and inferences. More importantly, this example shows that the very notion of observability is a matter of convention and hinges on the criteria we set for it to apply. (This also applies to substances and mixtures, in so far as they are understood in terms of a theory about what is elemental and what is compound.)

In any case, let us initially assume that unless the world is a construct of our minds, it is more or less plausible that the things we see, touch, smell and so on exist.[37] Specifically, assume that chemical substances and mixtures are real; that is, they exist independently of whether and how humans perceive them, and

---

[36] This does not mean that direct observation may not be distorted by how we observe the world via our senses. Colour blindness is an example.

[37] Whether directly observable stuff exists is an interesting question.

independently of how chemists describe them.[38] What about the chemical entities that are not directly observable through our senses, such as atoms, molecules, bonds, orbitals and so on?

Case V. Atoms and Molecules

Let's start with atoms and molecules. In the eighteenth century, Dalton postulated that atoms – that is, indivisible chunks of matter – make up different elements and combine to form molecules. While Dalton's theory of atoms allowed chemists to gain a better insight into elements and how they differ from each other, many chemists were sceptical as to their reality. This is partly because Dalton's theory contributed mostly by offering for the first time a visual representation of atoms. He used images and wooden balls to show how atoms combine to form molecules – something that Dalton himself considered more of a teaching tool than a depiction of reality (Ball 2021: 141). In general, up until the beginning of the twentieth century, scientists viewed atoms and molecules as hypothetical entities, leaving open the possibility that they have no ontological import and that they just help describe, predict and explain chemical and physical phenomena (Hendry 2018: 110).

This attitude is said to have changed with Perrin, who claimed to have empirically established the reality of atoms and molecules (1916). He supported this claim by illustrating how the same value for Avogadro's number can be calculated with relatively close agreement by thirteen different methods applied to a diverse range of phenomena (Nye 1972).[39] The domain of inquiry within which Perrin undertook his calculations was very broad as it included 'the measurement of the coefficient of diffusion; the mobility of ions; the blue color of the sky (the diffraction of the sunlight by the atmospheric molecules); the charge of ions; radioactive bodies; and the infrared part of the spectrum of the black-body radiation' (Psillos 2011: 355). Based on the empirical success of his analysis, Perrin stated:

> Our wonder is aroused at the very remarkable agreement found between values derived from the consideration of such widely different phenomena. Seeing that not only is the same magnitude obtained by each method when the conditions under which it is applied are varied as much as possible, but that the numbers thus established also agree among themselves, without discrepancy, for all the methods employed, the real existence of the molecule is given a probability bordering on certainty. (1916: 206–7)

---

[38] Admittedly, this is a very weak realist stance. Note that I say 'independent of how chemists call them' because I take this issue to fall under the question of natural kinds (discussed in Section 2).

[39] Avogadro's number (or constant) represents 'the molar number of entities' (IUPAC 2014: 133); that is, the number of entities (molecules, atoms, electrons etc.) in 1 gram-mole of a substance.

Agreement between calculations that were conducted within different domains of inquiry, and by employing different experimental methods, constituted empirical evidence that atoms and molecules are real. Perrin was subsequently awarded the Nobel Prize in Physics for establishing the 'physical existence' of those entities.[40]

It is no surprise that Perrin's work is discussed in the debate about scientific realism. Philosophers became particularly interested in spelling out Perrin's reasoning behind his claim that atoms and molecules are real. Salmon (1985), for instance, argues that Perrin's realist argument is an application of the Principle of the Common Cause. According to this principle, apparent coincidences are explained by the occurrence of a common cause (see Reichenbach 1956). Applied to the case in question, the fact that distinct calculations of Avogadro's number coincided on the same value is explained in virtue of a common cause; that is, the existence of the entities posited by the underlying theoretical hypothesis. Achinstein (2001), Chalmers (2011) and Psillos (2011) each take Perrin's realist claim to be an example of the 'robustness argument'. According to this argument, the 'empirical results indicate the reality of unobservables if these results are generated by a variety of empirical methodologies' (Hudson 2020: 34). On this view, the reality of unobservable entities is supported by the fact that diverse and different empirical methods produce the same value for Avogadro's number.[41]

On the other hand, van Fraassen argues that we should not interpret Perrin's work as establishing the reality of atoms and molecules, but as showing the empirical adequacy of the atomic and molecular hypothesis. This view is based on a more general anti-realist stance held by van Fraassen, called constructive empiricism. According to this, '(s)cience aims to give us theories which are empirically adequate; and acceptance of a theory involves as belief only that it is empirically adequate' (van Fraassen 1980: 12). In this context, the empirical evidence which is produced in support of a theory need not be construed as indicating the reality of that theory's unobservable entities, but only as supporting its empirical adequacy (van Fraassen 2009: 23). (This, of course, relies on some definition of the observable that does not allow atoms to count as such.)

Van Fraassen supports this argument for the case of atoms and molecules in large part through a historical analysis of the relevant scientific period. He claims that realists promote a distorted historical narrative of how scientists investigated and understood atoms and molecules in the eighteenth and

---

[40] This is stated on the Nobel Prize website: Jean Baptiste Perrin – Facts. NobelPrize.org. Nobel Prize Outreach AB 2022. Wed. 16 November 2022. www.nobelprize.org/prizes/physics/1926/perrin/facts/.

[41] Hudson (2020) argues that Perrin's reasoning should be understood as an instance of 'calibration' and not 'robustness'.

nineteenth centuries. Realists misinterpret scientists' views of the time by employing terms in their narratives that scientists themselves did not use or did not understand the way realists do today (namely, 'empirical adequacy') (2009: 7). Moreover, Perrin's models for the calculation of Avogadro's number were allegedly based on a problematic understanding of molecules as perfectly elastic and hard spheres – an assumption which scientists had already called into question due to Rutherford's insights on nuclear structure (Van Fraassen 2009: 8). All in all, he claims that realists exaggerate the ontological weight scientists (including Perrin) assigned to atoms and molecules.

Another challenge to the reality of atoms and molecules is the problem of unconceived alternatives. Duhem ([1914] 1991) noticed that theory choice often proceeds through eliminative reasoning: scientists choose among competing hypotheses or theories by eliminating those that they believe are less tenable. He pointed out that this eliminative reasoning can only be reliable in one's pursuit for the true theory if among the alternative theories considered there is the true one too. Following Duhem's reasoning, Stanford argues that history contains numerous instances in which scientists failed to conceive alternative theories that 'were both well confirmed by the evidence available at the time and sufficiently plausible as to be later accepted by actual scientific communities' (2006: 27). That is, we cannot be confident that among the theories that scientists conceive, the true theory is one of them. Therefore, eliminative reasoning is not reliable and we ought to be sceptical as to the truth of the theory that has been selected via elimination.

Stanford (2009) and Roush (2005) have debated whether this argument applies to atoms. Roush argues that in the case of Perrin's analysis, there weren't any other alternatives to the atomic hypothesis that could equally well explain Brownian motion.[42] On her view, the randomness of motion cannot be explained by anything else but the existence of particles. This is because a *random* Brownian motion implies the existence of particles that perform that motion (Roush 2005: 219). Note that unlike previous realist arguments, Roush's focus is not on all the phenomena that Perrin empirically examined to corroborate the atomic hypothesis. Rather the argument is that in the single case of Brownian motion, there are no other plausible theoretical hypotheses that could explain it. Therefore, the problem of unconceived alternatives doesn't arise.

Stanford makes two points against this argument. First, there were alternative hypotheses at the time (including the electromagnetic view of matter) which were considered plausible explanations of Brownian motion (Stanford 2009: 260). Second, eliminating the possibility of alternative hypotheses which

---

[42] Namely, the random, uncontrollable motion of particles in a medium (under certain conditions).

haven't been conceived is itself an instance of eliminative reasoning, which in turn is an unreliable method of argumentation. He purports that historically scientists have been often wrong when they assumed that there are no other ways to explain some phenomenon, and this is evidence that eliminative reasoning is unreliable. Given that Roush similarly bases her argument on eliminative reasoning, it follows that her conclusion is also unreliable, or so Stanford argues (2009: 262).

Hendry (2018) considers another chemical case where the problem of unconceived alternatives may apply. Since the 1860s, chemists have developed different representations of the spatial arrangements of atoms in molecules, called structural formulae. Different formulae were proposed over the decades (such as Kekulé's sausage formulae and Hofmann's glyphic formulae) with different explanatory and empirical aims (Hendry 2018: 110). The case of interest here is van't Hoff's representation of organic molecules which exhibited distinct stereoisomeric structures. The appropriate formulae had to depict the spatial arrangement of these molecules in such a way as to agree with the empirical information regarding the right number of isomers. To decide as to the appropriate structural formula, van't Hoff followed an eliminative reasoning: he considered alternative representations and eliminated those that he regarded less tenable. In this process, he chose a tetrahedral structure because it successfully differentiated between the right number of isomers. Had he selected the square planar arrangement, a surplus of alternative stereoisomeric structures would have been produced which was against empirical evidence.

This, according to Hendry, is an example of eliminative reasoning in chemistry which proved to be reliable. Its reliability was supported not only by the observations van't Hoff had readily available; it was further corroborated through the development and use of future spectroscopical and other experimental results (Hendry 2018: 114). So, in contrast to Stanford, whose analysis of historical episodes in science putatively illustrates the unreliability of eliminative reasoning, Hendry takes the analysis of alternative structural formulae in the nineteenth century to illustrate the reliability of eliminative reasoning in chemistry.[43]

This is not where the debate around realism in chemistry ends, far from it. Moving beyond atoms and molecules, it is worth looking at the general arguments formulated within the scientific realism debate, and present how our metaphysical understanding of chemistry has and can be further informed by such arguments.

---

[43] One could counter that this argument does not resolve the problem. In principle, it could still be the case that there are other unconceived ways to represent those structures which – unlike those eliminated – would not be discarded by empirical evidence.

Case VI. Phlogiston

The most characteristic defence of realism is via the No-Miracles Argument (NMA). As Putnam famously put it: 'the positive argument for realism is that it is the only philosophy that doesn't make the success of science a miracle' (1975: 73). Specifically, the reality of unobservable entities is supported by the argument that – were they not real – it would be miraculous that the theories which posit them are so successful in predicting and explaining phenomena. Put differently, the best explanation for the fact that our scientific theories are empirically successful is that they correctly identify the unobservable entities in the world (Ladyman 2012: 213).

One cannot deny that chemistry is a hugely successful science in terms of explanation and prediction. It accurately does both for the results of chemical reactions and the chemical properties of matter, through a constant process of experimental analysis via diverse methodologies. It has also contributed to the advancement of other sciences, including physics, biology, geology and astronomy. It has led to the development of applications in chemical engineering, medicine, nanotechnology and agriculture with enormous effects on our health and lifestyle. Chemists have predicted new phenomena, proposed novel applications and discovered (and also synthesised) previously unknown elements and substances. Following the NMA, it would be miraculous if chemistry had achieved all this and yet was wrong about the entities and properties that make all this happen.

Of objections to the NMA perhaps the most important is the Pessimistic Meta-Induction argument (PMI). According to Laudan (1981), the history of science offers several examples of theories which were at some point in time empirically successful but were later rejected or whose entities were discarded. Given that such revisions are quite common in the history of science, by induction one should expect that in the future the theories we regard as true today will be similarly revised or rejected. So, we are not justified in believing in the unobservable entities posited by our best current science.

To support the PMI, Laudan invoked an episode from the history of chemistry; namely, the Chemical Revolution (1981: 29). The Chemical Revolution refers to the period during which chemists abandoned the so-called phlogiston theory and accepted Lavoisier's theory of combustion. Until the eighteenth century, phlogistonists believed that combustion is the result of a principle or element called 'phlogiston'. The term was inspired by the Greek word for 'set on fire', and first posited in Stahl's theory of combustion articulated in 1703 (Ball 2021: 66–8). Very briefly, Stahl claimed that substances contain different amounts of phlogiston which are released into the air whenever these substances burn. This hypothesis was invoked to explain why matter weighed less after being burned, and why lighted candles in closed containers would eventually go out. Phlogiston was also supposed to explain other phenomena, including respiration and acidity, and it was posited by Stahl to be what all metals have in common, making them similar in their properties.[44]

For some time, the theory agreed quite well with empirical observations; however, disagreements with observations eventually accumulated (Blumenthal and Ladyman 2017). Among other things, chemists discovered that certain substances gained, instead of lost, weight when they burned – an empirical fact that contradicted the phlogiston theory. Eventually the phlogistonists started to disagree radically about how phlogiston related to the known behaviour of acids, bases, metals, salts and water, as well as to the growing list of newly discovered substances, including hydrogen, oxygen, carbon dioxide and nitric oxide. Around the same time in the 1780s, Lavoisier argued that there is no such thing as phlogiston and proposed an account of combustion according to which when substances burn, they absorb or combine with an element in the air which he called 'oxygen'.

This episode in chemistry is an example of how a previously successful theory posited something that was later rejected. As such it has been invoked as one of several episodes in the history of science during which scientists posited unobservable entities they later discarded. In this context, one raises a serious anti-realist worry about chemistry. Given that chemists at the time had sufficient empirical grounds to believe in the existence of phlogiston, how can we be sure that chemists today – who equally base their beliefs on empirical evidence – do not believe in fictitious entities?

There are different responses a realist could offer. First, one could argue that unlike today, chemistry during the time of the phlogistonists was not a mature science. What is today a thorough empirical practice was back then guided by outdated qualitative ideas inherited from Aristotle and the Renaissance period. It was not a mathematicised science and phlogistonists did not have the ability to precisely measure masses and volumes to corroborate their hypotheses (Ladyman 2011: 91). Given this, it is to be expected that past chemical theories were incorrect, and it would be unfair to generalise from this that modern chemistry will be equally false in the future. Chemistry today has undergone extensive empirical scrutiny and thorough experimental analysis; chemical hypotheses have been tested by multiple experimental techniques and with

---

[44] After Stahl's initial theory of phlogiston, multiple phlogiston theories emerged, each making slightly different claims about how phlogiston explains combustion and other phenomena. Eventually, some phlogistonists dropped the idea that all metals contain phlogiston (Blumenthal and Ladyman 2017).

growing precision.[45] So it is safe to believe that the entities posited by our current chemical theory of combustion, including oxygen, are real.

Another way to deal with the PMI is to admit that phlogiston is real; that is, it correctly refers to something in the world. Even if phlogistonists did not realise it, 'phlogiston' referred to at least some of the properties and causal powers that are responsible for combustion, respiration and calcination.[46] Accepting this allows us to be realists about our currently posited unobservable entities because it admits that past theories were in some sense correct as well, thus defeating the main idea of the PMI. However, it comes at a cost, as we not only have to admit that phlogiston is real but also do so in a way that is in danger of triviality. As Laudan (1984) points out, any past theoretical entity can be said to be real to the extent that we take it to refer to whatever it is that causes the relevant phenomena (regardless of whether we have discovered those causes or not).

A more nuanced response is to say that some parts of the phlogiston theory are true and other parts are false. The parts which are true have been retained in the newly accepted theory of combustion, whereas those that are false have been discarded. This sort of continuity between past and present theories allows us to circumvent the PMI and retain a realist stance. Psillos calls this the 'divide et impera move'. According to this view, 'when a theory is abandoned, its theoretical constituents ... should not be rejected en bloc' (Psillos 2005: 108). There are parts of those theories that were essential to their empirical success and – as such – are retained in our current theories. That this is plausible is supported by looking at the empirical success of the phlogiston theories. Indeed, phlogistonists were not completely wrong about everything and even made novel predictions, such as predict new acids which were subsequently retained by the new theory (Ladyman 2011: 99). So even though chemists today do not use the term 'phlogiston', the theory which posited it captured some aspects of the world correctly, even if partly. If we accept this claim, then this allows us to circumvent the PMI and thus be realists about currently posited unobservable entities.

Interestingly, there are disagreements about what exactly is retained from past to present theories and these disagreements produce different ontological commitments with respect to past theories. For example, Psillos claims that phlogiston as a material entity is not real as it was not essential to the theory. On this view, phlogiston 'refers to nothing'; that is, there is no material stuff in the

---

[45] Note that this is another way one can apply the 'robustness argument' to chemistry.

[46] This idea is developed as part of the causal theory of reference (e.g. Kripke 1972). How scientific terms refer is a semantic issue with important implications to our metaphysical understanding of the world. I do not delve into this.

world that possesses the properties assigned by phlogistonists to the entity called 'phlogiston' (Psillos 2005: 291).[47] Kitcher (1993) agrees that phlogiston doesn't refer to anything, but contends that 'dephlogisticated air', under some of its past usages, successfully referred to something in the world (namely, to what we call today 'oxygen').[48] Ladyman also believes that there is no thing released during combustion called phlogiston. However, he does not believe that phlogiston was inessential to the phlogiston theory of combustion. Instead, since (among other things) the theory was correct that ordinary combustion, the calcination of metals and respiration are all the same kind or process, it 'did to some extent correctly describe the causal or nomological structure of the world' (2011: 100). In this context, there is something real captured by the phlogiston theory, namely, modal structure, even though there is not a material entity released during combustion.[49]

By establishing some form of continuity between past and present chemical theories, several philosophers have responded to the PMI and thus retained their realism. However, there is also a different way to be a realist about chemical stuff which substantially diverges from the general spirit of the previous views. It is called `pragmatic realism'. On Chang's view, phlogiston is 'as real as tables-and-chairs and cats-and-dogs are in our daily lives' (2016: 118; also Chang 2012b). In fact, phlogiston is real in the same way that oxygen is, even though the two entities are posited by theories that are inconsistent with each other.[50]

While this seems like a strong metaphysical view in the sense of being ontologically committed to phlogiston, it substantially diverges from the traditional spirit of scientific realism. This is because it understands the truth of scientific theories in terms of coherentism. Standardly, coherentism takes truth to amount to nothing more than a set of propositions being logically consistent with each other (e.g. Austin 1962). The truth of a proposition is not defined by whether it corresponds to something in the world, but by whether it logically coheres with the rest of the propositions with which it is put together. Even though Chang follows the spirit of coherentism, he amends his understanding of

---

[47] This idea is part of the causal-descriptivist theory of reference (e.g. Psillos 2005).

[48] On the other side, when the term was used to denote 'the substance obtained when the substance emitted in combustion is removed from the air', it did not refer to anything because such a substance does not exist (Kitcher 1993: 102).

[49] This realist view is part of Ontic Structural Realism (OSR) according to which scientific theories correctly capture the modal relations and structures in the world (Ladyman and Ross 2007).

[50] They are logically and physically inconsistent because the oxygen theory of combustion explicitly denies that phlogiston exists and takes combustion to be the result of a completely different process than the phlogiston theories. Chang denies that they are logically inconsistent as they are incommensurable. On his view, we cannot compare them; therefore, the question of consistency is a non-starter. This is at odds with the fact that Lavoisier and others did compare them, and that many phlogistonists converted to the oxygen theory after such a comparison.

truth in his account of pragmatic realism. Specifically, he claims that truth is granted not to a set of propositions, but to a scientific practice which succeeds in meeting its aims. As he states: 'I define (pragmatist) coherence as a harmonious fitting-together of actions that leads to the successful achievement of one's aims' (2016: 112).

Based on this understanding of truth, Chang argues that phlogiston is real because it is part of a scientific practice which was very successful in achieving its aims. Not only did phlogistonists pursue a well-defined coherent set of aims (such as to phlogisticate or de-phlogisticate air) when they analysed the relevant phenomena, but they often considered these aims as being successfully met. Chang presents historical evidence that purportedly shows this to be the case. Based on this, he argues that to the extent that phlogistonists considered their practice a success, we should admit their theory as true and regard the entities which they posited as real.

There are two replies one can formulate against this view. First, one can deny that the aims set by phlogistonists were fulfilled or deemed successful by them. This objection is based on an examination of the history of phlogiston theories. Historical work has revealed that there were numerous disputes and empirical problems that phlogistonists faced and could not resolve in the context of their accepted theory (e.g. Blumenthal and Ladyman 2017, 2018). As Blumenthal and Ladyman argue, phlogiston theories eventually 'reached impasses due to internal problems or included features which made them unacceptable even to other phlogistians' (Blumenthal and Ladyman, 2018: 169). A second objection is that pragmatic realism misses what truth and realism are supposed to capture.[51] Even though Chang claims that phlogiston is real, the notion of reality that he advocates is far from the defining idea of realism; namely, that there is an external world in which there are things which exist independently of how we conceive them.

As a possible response to this last objection, we could invoke Chang's normative point about truth and reality. Chang argues that we should amend our notion of truth and realism and assign to them different meanings altogether. This is because traditional understandings of realism and truth are 'dead metaphors': we do not have access to the external world and thus we shouldn't take our descriptions of the world as literal (2016: 109–10). Now this is a perfectly admissible metaphysical view which is traditionally advocated by philosophers from the anti-realist camp.[52] The only difference with Chang's account is how this idea is branded. But regardless of how one wishes to define

---

[51] This criticism is based on a standard criticism to the coherentist theory of truth and is extended here to realism.

[52] The fact that Chang invokes ideas of Kant, Carnap, Cassirer and the Vienna Circle (i.e. thinkers that are paradigmatic of anti-realism) is indicative of his anti-realism (2016: 110, 120).

the terms 'realism' and 'truth', the case remains that under pragmatic realism one is not ontologically committed to the mind-independent existence of scientific entities or even to the existence of an external world. Put differently, the pursuit of discovering what exists in the world independently of us eludes pragmatic realism.

All in all, the analysis of scientific realism from the perspective of chemistry reveals something very interesting about our understanding of chemical ontology. If we want to claim that the entities chemists posit in their modern theories are real, we must account for the entities which chemists invoked in the past but now reject. We cannot have a complete metaphysical account based solely on modern chemistry; we also need to consider the historical evolution of chemical ontology.

But even this does not suffice to settle the reality of chemistry. The realist question is (at least) two dimensional. So far, I have sketched the first axis, which concerns the historical evolution of chemical ontology. The second axis concerns chemical constitution. In this context, I address the third question at the start of this section: should we believe in the reality of chemical entities given that they are composed of other (physical) things?

3.2 Chemistry's Relation to Quantum Physics

An old idea entertained to this day is that everything in the universe is made of just a few basic types of matter.[53] Despite the phenomenal diversity in nature and the apparent differences between clouds, rocks and chairs, everything is made of the same stuff. For a long time, people referred to this stuff as 'elements' or 'principles'. Opinions about what exactly these elements are like diverged throughout the centuries. For example, in ancient China, it was believed that they are water, fire, earth, wood and metal. In the sixteenth century, Paracelsus thought they were sulfur, salt and mercury (e.g. Brock 2012 for an overview). Boyle, who became to be known as the father of chemistry, believed that there are more elements than just three and defined them as:

> certain primitive and simple, or perfectly unmingled bodies; which not being made of other bodies, or of one another, are the ingredients of which all those called perfectly mixt bodies are immediately compounded, and into which they are ultimately resolved. (Boyle 2003: 141)

---

[53] Materialism is very crudely the idea that 'the only things that exist are those that occupy space' (Brown and Ladyman 2019: 3). Materialists deny the existence of immaterial stuff, like the spirit, the soul or a thinking substance. Materialism often (though not necessarily) includes the idea that few principles of matter constitute everything in the universe.

In the eighteenth century, Lavoisier offered an empirical criterion for identifying a chemical element, by defining it as 'a chemical substance that cannot be decomposed using current analytical methods' (Hendry 2005: 31). In the nineteenth century, chemistry's understanding of elements became more nuanced with Dalton's theory that each element corresponds to a different type of atom. While there was scepticism as to the reality of atoms, they were nevertheless understood as indivisible chunks of matter that explain why elements combine with each other (Ball 2021: 141).

To this day, the connection of elements to atoms is retained. However, the idea that atoms represent the fundamental constituents of matter inadvertently collapsed with the development of quantum physics. In the twentieth century, it was discovered that atoms are not indivisible entities: they are made of electrons, protons and neutrons which in turn are made of even smaller physical entities and interactions. From that point onwards, it became clear that chemistry is no longer part of the search for the fundamental constituents of matter.

Nevertheless, the question of how chemical entities are constituted by physical ones is still open. This is an important question not only in its own right but also because it can inform how in general things in the world – from planets to plants and bacteria – relate to physical stuff. Moreover, alternative answers as to the constitution of chemical entities imply alternative views as to their reality. Therefore, answering how chemical entities are made of physical stuff has significant implications to our general worldview.

I examine the question of chemical constitution by considering inter-theory relations.[54] Inter-theory relations are often relations between sciences that overlap in their domains of inquiry yet differ in the sets of entities they posit to describe those domains. For example, thermodynamics and statistical mechanics are both (partly) concerned with explaining the behaviour of gases. The former describes that behaviour by invoking properties such as temperature, pressure and volume, whereas the latter describes it by invoking the statistical generalisations concerning the molecules that make up a gas. The sets of entities posited by such pairs are standardly found in distinct scales of energy, length and/or time. Put crudely, the entities of one science are smaller (in length, time and/or energy) than those of the other. This is why philosophers often refer to those pairs as the higher- and lower-level theories.

When quantum physics was developed in the twentieth century, scientists started to believe that it could eventually explain all chemical phenomena. This is due to its ability to describe the interactions of the subatomic particles making

---

[54] 'Inter-theory relations' should not be conflated with Darden and Maull's 'interfield theories' (1977). While there may be similarities between the two notions that are worth investigating, this is not pursued.

up certain atoms and molecules, which became feasible by solving the Schrödinger equation. Heitler and London (1927) were the first to solve this equation for small atoms and molecules, and even managed to identify quantum mechanically the covalent bonds of a hydrogen molecule. It was on this basis that Dirac exclaimed that:

> [t]he underlying physical laws necessary for the mathematical theory of a large part of physics and the whole of chemistry are thus completely known, and the difficulty is only that the exact application of these laws leads to equations much too complicated to be soluble. (1929: 714)

The actual and expected capabilities of quantum physics prompted questions about how to interpret chemistry's relation to physics. In fact, it is not surprising that, during the same period and for several decades after Dirac's notorious statement, philosophers of science proposed detailed accounts of reductionism (Carnap 1928/1967; Hempel 1966; Nagel 1979; Oppenheim and Putnam 1958). Reductionism is the idea that physics is somehow prior to or more fundamental than the other sciences, including chemistry. There are two ways one can interpret this claim: epistemically and metaphysically.[55] Different forms of epistemic and metaphysical reductionism are available, but the first model of reduction that was defended for the case of chemistry was formulated by Nagel (1979).[56]

According to Nagel, a theory is reduced to another when the theoretical statements of the former can logically derive those of the latter. If the vocabularies of the two theories are not identical, then derivability is made possible with the additional postulation of bridge laws; that is, statements that relate the concepts of the two theories. Nagel's reductionism is epistemological as it posits a relation between scientific descriptions and their respective concepts. Nevertheless, it is often thought that it has metaphysical implications. Given that bridge laws establish relations between concepts of higher and lower-level entities, it can be inferred that higher-level entities are substituted (and thus eliminated) by the lower-level entities to which they are connected via bridge laws.

---

[55] Epistemic forms of reduction focus on how the statements, descriptions or theories of two sciences relate. Metaphysical forms of reduction focus on how the entities posited by two sciences relate. Initially, philosophers did not distinguish between epistemic and metaphysical accounts, producing proposals that advocated both an epistemic and metaphysical reductive relation between two sciences (e.g. Nagel 1979; Oppenheim and Putnam 1958).

[56] Nagel did not so much explain why chemistry is reduced to quantum physics but rather claimed that his proposed model of reduction successfully applies to chemistry. Such dialectics were later criticised by philosophers of chemistry on the grounds that they overlook the precise details of chemistry.

The question of reductionism in chemistry is considered of perennial importance to the philosophy of chemistry. It is one of the most discussed topics since
the formation of this field as an organised discipline, and it has prompted
ideologically driven views around (and against) reductionism (Chang 2015a;
Lombardi and Labarca 2005; Scerri and Fisher 2016). This is because the
rejection of chemistry's reduction has been considered fundamental for the
survival of chemistry and of the philosophy of chemistry. As Lombardi and
Labarca state:

> This traditional assumption (of reduction) not only deprives the philosophy of
> chemistry of legitimacy as a field of philosophical inquiry, but also counts
> against the autonomy of chemistry as a scientific discipline: whereas physics
> turns out to be a 'fundamental' science that describes reality in its deepest
> aspects, chemistry is conceived as a mere 'phenomenological' science, that
> only describes phenomena as they appear to us. (2005: 126)

Such a stance towards chemistry's reduction may come as a surprise. How two
sciences relate is a matter of identifying whether there is a relation between
certain things, and correctly spelling out the main features of that relation.
And while this demands an analysis of the concepts employed to characterise
such a relation, what decides our views on that relation is (and should be)
based on an investigation of the relevant sciences. The survival of the philosophy of chemistry – or of chemistry for that matter – should not influence
how we understand the relation between scientific entities.

On the other hand, how we perceive the relation of things in the world can
affect the importance we assign to those things. From the reductionist perspective, physics is often perceived as a more fundamental science in that it uncovers
the true or ultimate nature of things. Nagel himself took reductionism's goal to
be the formulation of 'a comprehensive theory which will integrate all domains
of natural science in terms of a common set of principles' (1979: 336).
Advocating that everything is reduced to physics can be viewed as providing
legitimacy to physics over the other sciences and has been invoked to illustrate
its ontological priority. Moreover, as Cat (2022) points out, such considerations
can have practical consequences, influencing funding policies, decision-making
and science teaching.

However, there are also other factors that influence the existence and legitimacy of a scientific discipline. In this case, chemistry has immense financial
and social utility due to its role in the development of technology, the food
industry and medicine (among other sectors). This is key to understanding its
development in the educational and industrial sector. Research projects are
funded based on their explicit societal impact, and chemical academic curricula

are in tune with chemistry's utility. So, it seems quite unlikely that an adherence to chemistry's reduction will in fact threaten its existence, as some claim.[57]

Similarly, it is mistaken to believe that chemistry's reduction could render illegitimate the philosophy of chemistry as a field of study, as for example Scerri and Fisher believe (2016: 3). Granted, it took a while to establish it as a separate field (almost seventy years since philosophy of science was officially organised) and philosophers often seem to put more importance on the study of physics and biology when examining philosophical questions.[58] But chemistry always figured in philosophical discussions around science, even before an organised discipline was put together in the 1990s. Moreover, even if chemistry is reduced to physics, this does not render all other philosophical questions about chemistry moot. There are philosophical issues that can be informed by chemistry despite its alleged reduction, including epistemological and methodological ones. Also, as this Element illustrates, chemistry's reduction far from settles other metaphysical questions about chemistry.

This brings me to another point that has not been adequately clarified in the literature. An interesting feature of discussions around chemistry's reduction is the putative effect reductive views have on our realist position about chemistry. It is often mistakenly assumed by antireductionists about chemistry that advocating the reduction of chemistry necessitates or implies that chemical entities are not real (e.g. Lombardi and Labarca 2005: 134).[59] This may explain why chemistry's reduction is viewed as a threat towards its autonomy. And while indeed there is a version of reductionism that advocates the elimination of reduced entities from our ontology (i.e. eliminative reduction), there are also views that adhere to the ideal of unity yet maintain the reality of special science entities (more on this in Section 3.3). Moreover, even versions of reduction which purport an identity relation between higher and lower-level entities do not imply the elimination of higher-level entities. In fact, it is often argued that such a reduction requires the reality of the reduced ontology (e.g. van Riel and van Gulick 2019). This is because metaphysical reductionism is generally committed to the reality of the reducing entities. From this, it follows that the things which are identical to reducing entities are real as well.

---

[57] Chang states: 'the relationship between physics and chemistry is one of the perennial foundational issues in the philosophy of chemistry. It concerns the very existence and identity of chemistry as an independent scientific discipline' (2015a: 193).

[58] This is shown, for instance, by the disproportionate number of articles and talks in major philosophy of science journals and conferences that focus on physics and biology compared to those focusing on chemistry.

[59] To be fair, initial accounts of reduction (Kemeny and Oppenheim 1956; Nagel 1979) did claim or imply a form of eliminativism about reduced entities.

In any case, talk of how chemical entities relate to physical ones influences the investigation of the realist question about chemistry, in more ways than one. To illustrate this, I present the main antireductionist argument about chemistry; present two central metaphysical views that have been prompted by this argument; and show how each account involves a realist claim about chemistry.

Case VII. Molecular Structure

Quantum physics is taken to describe the properties of atoms and molecules by solving the Schrödinger equation. The Schrödinger equation calculates the interactions of each and every subatomic particle that makes up a system. From this it is possible to derive the system's observable properties, including its chemical ones. While this could prima facie serve as evidence that chemistry is reduced (in Nagel's sense) to quantum physics, philosophers of chemistry have argued against this. This is because quantum physics does not satisfy a supposedly key requirement for Nagelian reductionism; namely, that derivability is realised from first principles.[60]

Derivability is not realised from first principles because in practice a solution to the Schrödinger equation always involves making idealisations and approximations to the equation. These idealisations and approximations have a physical justification and are based on prior empirical knowledge of the system and its chemistry. Nevertheless, they are taken to suggest the irreducibility of chemistry. This is because, had they not been used, quantum physics would have been unable to produce the expected results about the system.

The most characteristic example invoked to illustrate this is molecular structure. Molecular structure refers to the spatial arrangement of the atoms that constitute a molecule. The quantum mechanical identification of a molecule's structure is standardly achieved after implementing the Born-Oppenheimer approximation (BO) to the Schrödinger equation. Applying this approximation results in a quantum mechanical representation 'of the complete wavefunction as a product of an electronic and a nuclear part where the two wave-functions may be determined separately by solving two different Schroedinger equations' (IUPAC 2014: 179). This amounts to disregarding the interactions that take place between a system's nuclei.[61]

The use of the BO approximation putatively supports the irreducibility of chemistry for three reasons. First, the assumptions that are made via this

---

[60] I say 'supposedly' because one can challenge the view that derivability has to occur from first principles. I do not examine this.

[61] The approximation is justified 'on the fact that the ratio of electronic to nuclear mass (...) is sufficiently small and the nuclei, as compared to the rapidly moving electrons, appear to be fixed' (IUPAC 2014: 179).

approximation are structural (Hendry 2012b: 373; Woolley 1976). The BO 'fixes' the nuclei in space and thus presupposes a particular position for them. This means that one assumes and imposes some structural information to the equation, before identifying the overall structure of the system. Second, the structural information that is transcribed via the BO approximation is drawn from the chemical examination of the system (Hendry 2012b; Scerri 1998). This means that the higher-level theory has been used to presuppose information in the lower-level description. Third, these assumptions are putatively necessary for the identification of structure; they are not merely an indication of an inability to solve a very complicated equation (Hendry 2010: 186; Woolley and Sutcliffe 1977). Even if it were possible to solve the equation without applying the BO approximation, the relevant solution would not identify any structure to the system (more on this later in this section). This suggests that quantum physics is *in principle* unable to identify chemical properties; that is, quantum physics alone cannot derive chemical properties.

As already mentioned, some philosophers argue that this is evidence of the failure of chemistry's Nagelian reduction (Scerri 1994). Others argue that it is evidence that chemical entities are somehow distinct or autonomous from the physical entities that make them up (see the following paragraphs). I do not critically analyse the arguments against the epistemic reduction of chemistry. Instead, I focus on the metaphysical implications that are drawn (at least in part) from this antireductionist argument.

There are two metaphysical views that have been proposed: strong emergence and ontological pluralism. Strong emergence claims that the use of the BO approximation for the identification of molecular structure is evidence that structure is a strongly emergent property (Hendry 2010, 2012b). There are three features to this view which specify the precise form of strong emergence that is advocated by Hendry.[62] First, in line with other emergentist accounts, there is a hierarchy of levels. Nature is divided into distinct energy, length and time scales within which different entities are found. Second, structure depends on the interactions of the subatomic entities which make up the molecule. Hendry spells out this dependence in terms of supervenience (2010: 185). Very briefly, structure (just like any chemical property) supervenes on the relevant quantum physical entities and their interactions in the sense that whenever there is a change in a molecule's structure there is also some change in the quantum physical entities of that molecule. Third, structure is causally autonomous. There are different ways one can spell out causal autonomy (e.g. Wilson 2016). In the context of Hendry's account, structure is causally autonomous in

---

[62] My analysis of Hendry's position on strong emergence is based on Seifert 2020.

the sense that it possesses causal powers that are not token identical to any set of powers of the relevant quantum physical entities. This is further spelled out in terms of downward causation. That is, structure possesses downward causal powers: it partly causes the way in which the subatomic particles of the molecule interact with each other (Hendry 2010: 185).

While Hendry argues for strong emergence only for the case of molecular structure, his overall framework and its subsequent metaphysical implications produces a very interesting image of chemical ontology. On his view, a molecule's structure is not ontologically reducible to its lower-level physical parts: structure is not identical to, nor the complete result of interactions among the molecule's physical parts. Instead, structure is a distinct property which doesn't exist at the scale where quantum physical entities are found; it exists at a different scale (Hendry 2010: 186)

Moreover, structure is said to have a downward causal effect on how the molecule's physical constituents behave. Just like the movements of every participant in a sirtaki dance is partially determined by the geometry and rhythms that a sirtaki adheres to, so the interactions of each subatomic particle are determined by the overall structure of the entire system. It is in virtue of the ability to exert downward causal powers – that is, to causally influence the lower-level constituents – that structure is distinct and non-reducible to its physical parts. This implies that strong emergence makes for a realist position about higher-level entities. If one accepts Alexander's dictum that *to be is to cause,* then it follows that molecular structure is real.[63]

The second metaphysical account is ontological pluralism. Lombardi and Labarca take the inability of quantum mechanics to identify a molecule's structure as suggestive of chemistry's autonomy. They spell out chemistry's autonomy in terms of ontological pluralism; that is, the thesis that 'permits the coexistence of different but equally objective theory-dependent ontologies interconnected by nomological, non-reductive relationships' (2005: 146). Based on Putnam's internalist realism, they reject that there is an external world to which we can gain access via our scientific descriptions. Instead, the world and its objects are dependent on how we perceive and conceptualise them. Put differently, the world is contingent on and determined by the theory within which we describe it, rejecting what is standardly called the 'God's eye view', which purportedly discovers the objective, mind-independent world.[64]

There are several implications of their view. First, there is no external world that one aims at discovering (as per traditional scientific realism). Instead, there

---

[63] One could question the tenability of Alexander's dictum.

[64] Their idea of chemical autonomy is largely inspired by Kant's philosophy.

is a plurality of ontologies which can be inconsistent to each other yet carry the same ontological weight (i.e. they are all equally real). In the case in question, the entities postulated by quantum physics 'co-exist' with those of chemistry. There is no metaphysical priority of physical entities over chemical ones. Physical entities are not more fundamental. There is no hierarchical relation between the chemical and physical levels, as accepted by Hendry's strong emergence or by the standard hierarchical image introduced by Oppenheim and Putnam (1958).

There are conceptual and empirical challenges to both strong emergence and ontological pluralism. One conceptual issue with strong emergence is how exactly to understand causation when talking of downward causation. Given the multiplicity of causal accounts in terms of production, counterfactuals or mechanisms, it is an open question which (if any) of these accounts fit in the context of Hendry's strong emergence (see Seifert 2020: 23). Another issue has to do with whether downward causation is a synchronic or diachronic relation between a cause and its effect (Seifert 2020: 5–11). This is important because some philosophers argue that synchronic causation is incoherent: an effect cannot occur at exactly the same moment that the cause occurs (e.g. Kim 1999).[65] With respect to ontological pluralism, it is not entirely clear how it understands the dependence relation between a molecule and its parts. If we understand chemistry and quantum physics as offering distinct ontological pictures of the world, then how can we make sense of connections that the relevant sciences advocate for them?[66]

From an empirical perspective, strong emergence and ontological pluralism face a common challenge.[67] Can the use of the BO approximation be interpreted in ways that do not require the postulation of downward causes or distinct ontologies? If so, then both antireductionist views are undermined by adhering to Occam's razor. According to this principle, 'a theory that postulates few entities, processes, or causes is better than a theory that postulates more, so long as the simpler theory is compatible with what we observe' (Sober 2015: 2). In this context, if there is a metaphysical view that is more parsimonious compared to strong emergence and ontological pluralism, then it should be preferred.

Indeed, there is evidence towards that direction. Franklin and Seifert (2020) point out that the use of the BO approximation is a result of the measurement problem in quantum mechanics. The measurement problem arises because quantum physics predicts certain systems to be in superposition states relative to a measurement basis even though the measurement of those states produces

---

[65] Others argue that synchronic causation is coherent (see Friend 2019).

[66] Hettema raises a similar worry (2017: 237).

[67] I leave open whether these are the only challenges that can be raised.

determinate outcomes. If we assume that the Schrödinger equation offers a complete description of a quantum state, this reveals an apparent inconsistency, which is referred to as the measurement problem (e.g. Maudlin 1995).

According to Franklin and Seifert (2020), the measurement problem is central to understanding why the BO approximation is used for the identification of molecular structure. Without applying the approximation, quantum physics predicts that the ground state of certain types of molecules corresponds to a superposition of their structures.[68] For example, this is the case with optical isomers: their predicted ground state corresponds to a superposition of all their possible isomeric structures. Given that we only observe a determinate structure, and that the quantum physical description of isomers is assumed to be complete, it follows that this is an instance of the measurement problem. Therefore, Franklin and Seifert conclude that the apparent inability of quantum physics to identify molecular structure from first principles is a special case of the measurement problem.

In light of this, different avenues become available to interpret quantum physics' apparent inability to identify structure (also referred to as the problem of molecular structure). By identifying the problem of molecular structure as a special case of the measurement problem, it follows that a solution to the measurement problem constitutes a solution to the problem of molecular structure. To this day, there is no consensus as to what the solution to the measurement problem is. Nevertheless, several solutions have been proposed in the context of alternative interpretations (and theories) of quantum mechanics, including the Copenhagen interpretation, the many-worlds interpretation and the de Broglie–Bohm theory. In this context, the crucial question becomes whether an adherence to any of these interpretations allows one to adopt a more parsimonious view of chemical ontology that does not require positing distinct ontologies (as per ontological pluralism) or downward causal powers (as per strong emergence).[69]

Another interesting result produced by Franklin and Seifert's thesis is that we need to distinguish between isolated and non-isolated systems when discussing how systems relate to their constituents (2020: 2; also Seifert 2020, 2022a). The case of structure is quite revealing of this as certain quantum physical interpretations suggest that structure may not be instantiated by isolated molecules; it only arises after interaction with some environment. If this is the case, then the question of reduction and emergence becomes moot for the case of isolated systems. If there is no structure for quantum

---

[68] The ground state corresponds to the stable observable state of a system.

[69] Franklin and Seifert claim that three standard realist interpretations to quantum mechanics undermine – in different ways each – the strong emergence of molecular structure (2020: 24–30).

physics to derive (in isolated systems), then strictly speaking there is no apparent inability of quantum physics to identify structure (as purported by antireductionism). This could render a very large part of the empirical basis for antireductionism out of place.

Admittedly, this is a brief discussion of how considerations around quantum physics can affect metaphysical questions about chemistry. Nevertheless, an analysis of quantum mechanics is crucial to formulating an empirically well-informed account of how chemistry and quantum physics relate. Thus, a metaphysics of quantum physics goes hand in hand with a cogent metaphysics of chemistry.

3.3 Unity and Realism, All in One

Another counterproposal to ontological pluralism and strong emergence which can retain (in different senses and degrees) the spirit of reductionism is to advocate for so-called unity. The unity of science is 'an ontological ideal – the thought that there is something that connects the various entities in reality, for instance, by way of one thing being composed of various other things' (Tahko 2021: 1). To understand the 'ideal of unity' contrast it with disunity. Disunity (in its ontological form) is the idea that the entities posited by different sciences are in some substantial way autonomous and independent of each other. On this view, even if some entities are in some way composed of other entities, they are still independent or even completely autonomous of the parts that make them up.[70] This independence can be spelled out in various ways, including in terms of strong emergence or pluralism.

Unity is often used as an umbrella term that encompasses many accounts, each specifying differently how the ideal of unity is achieved. Among these accounts, Nagelian reductionism is a paradigmatic example.[71] Another is physicalism. Physicalism is the view that everything is constituted of physical stuff (e.g. Kim 2007; Papineau 2002).[72] Again here we find different accounts of physicalism, including supervenience physicalism, realisation physicalism, determination physicalism and grounding (see Stoljar 2022 for an overview). Some philosophers distinguish between reductive physicalism and non-reductive physicalism.[73] In general, there are different flavours of physicalism

---

[70] I disregard epistemological or methodological accounts of (dis)unity.

[71] Similarly with disunity, which is an umbrella term for different and diverse accounts. Strong emergence and ontological pluralism are among those.

[72] Physicalism is often viewed as the modern version of materialism that was presented at the beginning of this section (see Brown and Ladyman 2019).

[73] This is just a suggestive classification of existing views as philosophers often classify or call them differently.

and different concepts employed to spell it out.[74] While this can make the discussion quite confusing, it also suggests that there are many ways to spell out how chemical and physical stuff relate.

Surprisingly, the philosophy of chemistry is not particularly informed by the unity and physicalist views that are available in the literature. Apart from a few philosophers who advocate some form of (mainly epistemological) reductionism, there is little else (see Hettema 2017; Needham 2010). (Only Le Poidevin (2005) advocates for the ontological reducibility of chemical elements.[75]) This is a clear lacuna, especially if we compare this discussion with the variety of unificatory accounts that are applied to biology and economics (e.g. Kincaid 1997; Papineau 2002).

What are the motivations to consider unity of any form for chemistry? If we wish to support metaphysical views on the basis of empirical evidence, then we cannot dismiss the evidence which is suggestive of unity in this particular case. Chemistry and quantum physics are not just logically consistent to each other, nor do they merely overlap in their domains of inquiry. The existence of quantum chemistry – that is, of 'a sub-discipline that is not quite physics, not quite chemistry, and not quite applied mathematics' – indicates that there are substantial epistemological relations that suggest their unity (Gavroglu and Simões 2011: viii).[76]

First, there are heuristic interconnections. Both sciences have enriched and influenced the research questions addressed by the other science with enormous empirical success to both. Tools, methods and models developed within chemistry have contributed to the investigation of research questions in quantum physics and vice versa (Seifert 2017: 218). For example, chemists have revised their understanding of atomic structure and transformed the chemical research around atoms and molecules due to the developments in quantum physics (see Pullman 2001). They have gained quantitative and qualitative information on molecular structure by employing quantum models for different types of atoms and molecules. Techniques in quantum chemistry have offered accurate descriptions of small molecules, polyatomic molecules and metals (Hoffman 1990). Quantum physics has revealed novel factors that affect our understanding of bonding,

---

[74] Physicalism can be viewed as a universal thesis (that everything is constituted of physical stuff), or a local thesis (that everything chemical or biological or etc. is constituted of physical stuff).

[75] His claim is based on the 'combinatorial criterion for ontological reduction' according to which 'a property type F is ontologically reducible to a more fundamental property type G if the possibility of something's being F is constituted by a recombination of actual instances of G, but the possibility of something's being G is not constituted by a recombination of actual instances of F' (Le Poidevin 2005: 132). He applies this criterion to claim that chemical elements and their ordering in the periodic table are reduced to their quantum physical entities and their interactions.

[76] Quantum chemistry is the field that applies quantum models for the description, prediction and explanation of chemical phenomena.

prompting debates around its nature that continue to this day (e.g. Song et al. 2019; Zhao et al. 2019). The two sciences' heuristic interdependence is also extended to a range of chemical sub-disciplines where quantum physical models are used, such as material science and drug design (Matta 2013: 245).

Second, the two sciences depend on each other in their processes of confirmation and prediction. The quantitative results of quantum models are compared with experimental results from chemistry to evaluate the accuracy of these models, and determine what changes are required to minimise error (Seifert 2017: 219). These experimental results are provided through the work of experimental chemists who, via spectroscopical and other techniques, calculate chemical properties.

Moreover, novel predictions of chemical phenomena have been made with the help of quantum physics. The specification of atomic structure by quantum physics helped chemists predict novel elements in accordance with the periodic table (Needham 2004: 213). Also, quantum models have made novel predictions about pericyclic reactions, large molecules and metals (Hendry 2004: 1057). These predictions enriched chemical knowledge and contributed to the confirmation of chemistry's theoretical posits. Overall, the results of chemical experimentation play a vital role in the development and evaluation of quantum models and vice versa.

Third, the two sciences are explanatorily interdependent in the following sense. Advances in quantum physics have enriched chemical explanations of molecular behaviour and even led to their revision. Conversely, chemical explanations have been used in the development of quantum models and have guided quantum chemists towards a more accurate interpretation of the mathematical description of atoms and molecules. In fact, explanatory differences both between different quantum models and between quantum models and chemistry have raised discussions to consolidate or review their explanatory accounts (Seifert 2017: 220).

For example, due to quantum physics chemists now have a mechanism that helps explain atomic structure in terms of electron configuration, which in turn explains the periodic classification of elements (Seifert 2017: 220). Moreover, quantum physics has contributed to chemistry's explanations of molecular structure. The development of the molecular orbital (MO) approach in quantum physics has revealed the effect of electron delocalisation on the stability of molecules. Within the framework of the MO approach, computational models such as the Hartree–Fock method and the Configuration Interaction approach take into account the repulsion of electrons, the ionic character of chemical bonds and the mixing of higher energy states, thus enriching chemistry's understanding of molecular structure (Weisberg 2008: 939–43). A similar interdependence is noticed in the case of chemical bonds. While chemists primarily understood the bond as a pair-wise relation among specific atoms in a molecule, quantum physics revealed the importance of delocalisation effects, illustrating that bonding is to some degree a molecular-wide phenomenon (Weisberg 2008). Another example concerns chemical reactions. Recently, it was discovered that quantum tunnelling can influence reaction pathways for certain isomers (Cláudio et al. 2022). Conversely, quantum models that are employed for explaining properties of complex atoms and molecules have been calibrated or corrected due to theoretical assumptions and explanations in chemistry (Hendry 2010: 183).

All in all, chemistry and quantum physics are intertwined in several ways. These interconnections are epistemic; they concern how two scientific practices relate to each other. As such, they can be invoked as evidence for an epistemic relation between the two sciences. They can also be invoked as evidence for their unity. For example, one could argue that the best explanation of these interconnections is that analogous metaphysical connections exist between the entities posited by chemistry and quantum physics. Put differently, these interconnections would be in some sense mysterious if the relevant ontologies of the two sciences are radically distinct and autonomous from each other.[77] To further support this abductive argument, one could add that these interconnections accumulate in time: throughout the historical development of chemistry and quantum physics, one identifies growing epistemic interconnections that continue to develop to this day and which offer further inductive support for the unity of the relevant ontologies. Note that this argument is not novel: it has been formulated by, for example, Kincaid 1997 for economics.

Nevertheless, this argument – being inductive – does not guarantee that these epistemological interconnections will persist. It is in principle possible that in the future quantum physics no longer connects with chemistry in a heuristic, explanatory or confirmatory manner. However, to the extent that we accept inductive reasoning in science as reliable, it is perfectly admissible to support unity by induction as well.

A more pressing shortcoming with this argument for unity is that it does not posit a specific form of unity; it merely suggests that the ideal of unity is more plausible than disunity when it comes to chemistry and quantum physics. Much more needs to be said about the form of dependence that holds within the framework of unity. For example, one could invoke standard physicalist

---

[77] This is a convincing argument against accounts that advocate the existence of radically distinct and independent ontologies (like ontological pluralism). It does not suffice to challenge disunity accounts that admit the existence of some dependence relation between chemical and quantum physical entities (such as strong emergence).

accounts and specify that relation in terms of supervenience (e.g. Papineau 2002). But supervenience is not particularly informative here: it merely states that whenever the higher-level entities change, there is also some change in their lower-level constituents. In fact, recall that supervenience is accepted by (some) disunity accounts about chemistry, namely strong emergence. So, a much more precise metaphysical account of dependence is required to substantiate the unity of chemistry with quantum physics. A case that could offer novel insight into how to spell out such an account is the chemical bond.

Case VIII. Chemical Bonds

Given that the available accounts on unity are under-explored in the philosophy of chemistry, the view which I present is only one way to support unity and reflects my own views on how to understand it with respect to chemistry. Specifically, I focus on the chemical bond and argue that bonds are related to their physical constituents in the sense that they are real patterns of interactions among subatomic particles (Seifert 2022b). This understanding of chemical bonds offers a way of defending their reality while maintaining the ideal of unity.

The idea that bonds exist when atoms form stable independent molecular entities has been of perennial importance to understanding chemical transformation and the properties of matter (IUPAC 2014: 257). Despite its value to science, there is a persisting debate in science and philosophy about the bond's nature and reality (Weisberg 2008: 932–3). To this day, scientific papers are published that try to understand what bonds are (e.g. Song et al. 2019; Zhao et al. 2019). Diverse views have been proposed as to whether bonds refer to material things, energetic facts or mere fictions. Lewis (who first posited covalent bonds) took a strong ontological stance about bonds when he said that 'in the mind of the organic chemist the chemical bond is no mere abstraction; it is a definite physical reality, a something that binds atom to atom' ([1923] 1966: 67). On the other hand, Coulson took the development of quantum models to show that bonds are nothing but mere fictions. He stated that 'a chemical bond is not a real thing: it does not exist: no-one has ever seen it, no-one ever can. It is a figment of our own imagination' (Coulson 1955: 2084).

In light of all this, Hendry (2008) proposes two alternative conceptions to the chemical bond: the energetic and the structural. The energetic conception takes bonds to refer to molecular-wide phenomena that correspond to states of energetic stabilisation of a molecule (Hendry 2008: 919). The structural conception takes bonds to be 'material parts' that are localised between pairs of atoms and are responsible for those atoms' pair-wise relation (Hendry 2008: 917).

While both conceptions offer valuable insights as to the nature of chemical bonds, neither makes clear what the dependence relation is between a bond and its physical parts, nor whether the bond is real. Under the structural conception, the chemical bond is 'responsible for spatially localized submolecular relationships between individual atomic centers', suggesting that it is real (Hendry 2008: 917). Nevertheless, this statement does not involve any claims about whether bonds conform to the ideal of unity. On the other hand, the energetic conception is compatible with understanding bonding both as a property of the entire molecule, and as a fictitious entity (Seifert 2022b: 13). So, the question about the reality of bonds remains open.

Understanding bonds as real patterns answers both questions. First, it specifies the dependence relation in terms of the notion of patterns. Second, it advocates that bonds are real. These claims are based on an idea formulated by Dennett (1991) and later adopted – with certain additions – by ontic structural realists (e.g. Ladyman and Ross 2007; Ross 2000).

Very briefly, Dennett's account is the following. A system may be described by various methods, some of which are more efficient than others. Among them is the least efficient method of describing the system called the 'bit map'. Efficiency can be understood in different ways, but for sake of brevity I understand it in terms of degrees of freedom (Ladyman 2017: 157; also Seifert 2022b: 21). Specifically, a description is more efficient than another if fewer independent parameters need to be specified to produce that description, compared to the number of parameters required for the other. In this context, a pattern exists if there is a way of describing a system that is more efficient than the bit map. This pattern is identified via the concepts employed by the more efficient description.[78]

For example, consider a collection of black and white dots. Its bit map is the description which identifies the position of each and every black and white dot (Dennett 1991: 32). However, suppose also that the black dots can be viewed as forming shapes in the frame, such as a series of black boxes. This makes it possible, instead of counting each and every black and white dot, to describe the frame by identifying the size and distance of the black boxes. Such a description would be more efficient than formulating the bit map because it requires specifying fewer variables. Following Dennett, this suffices to claim that there

---

[78] The most common objection to this is that there can be many descriptions that are more efficient than the bit map, thus raising the question whether we should regard all of them as (equally) real. This in turn has lead to instrumentalist and pluralist interpretations of patterns (e.g. Brading 2010; Fodor 1985). For a reply to these criticisms in the context of chemical bonds, see Seifert 2022: 28–34.

is a pattern in the way the black and white dots are positioned. Put boldly, the black boxes are (real) patterns of black dots in the frame.[79]

Dennett's account successfully applies to molecules (Seifert 2022: 16–18). The bit map description of a molecule corresponds to solving its Schrödinger equation from first principles. This is because solving this equation requires identifying the interactions of each and every electron and the nucleus that comprises the molecule, without disregarding any of the entities or interactions. Moreover, in quantum chemistry and chemistry, a molecule is described by more efficient methods than this. In quantum chemistry, the use of approximations and idealisations reduces the degrees of freedom of the quantum models employed to describe molecular systems. The implementation of the BO approximation alone suffices to support this, as this approximation amounts to disregarding the interactions among the nuclei of a system. Similarly, chemistry has fewer degrees of freedom compared to the bit map because it describes molecules in terms of the number and types of bonds that form between its atoms. This involves the specification of the electronic configuration of the atoms in a molecule which in turn is based on an analysis of only those electrons that are found in the atoms' outer shells.

This allows us to claim that chemical bonds are patterns of interactions between subatomic particles. This is because the more efficient descriptions employed in chemistry and quantum chemistry invoke bonds to describe molecules. In the process of describing the subatomic interactions of a molecule, quantum models (employed in quantum chemistry) identify chemical bonds in terms of electron clouds, bond paths or electron charge distributions (e.g. Macedo and Haiduke 2020). In chemistry, the number and types of bonds that are posited among specific atoms (such as covalent, ionic and metallic bonds) are central to the specification of a molecule and its structure. Therefore – like the boxes of black dots – bonds are real patterns.

While Dennett's account has been criticised on the basis of implying instrumentalism or pluralism about patterns, it has also been used as a way to understand the dependence of higher-level entities to lower-level ones. Ontic Structural Realism (OSR) as formulated by Ladyman and Ross adopts Dennett's idea of patters to offer an account of non-reductive unity which maintains the reality of higher-level entities.[80] On this view, descriptions

---

[79] Dennett uses 'existence' and 'being real' interchangeably, so in the present context they are understood as conveying the same idea (1991: 34).

[80] I disregard French's (2014) account as it is eliminativist with respect to higher-level entities. Also, Ladyman and Ross' account has prompted criticisms regarding its tenability as a universal thesis (e.g. Frigg and Votsis 2011). Given that I only consider this account for the case of bonds, I disregard them.

identify real patterns not only because they are more efficient than the bit map but also because they make counterfactual and nomological generalisations that successfully explain and predict phenomena (Ladyman 2017: 154).

Indeed, bonds satisfy this criterion. By positing, for instance, covalent bonds, chemistry makes counterfactual and nomological generalisations about how classes of molecules react and form stable entities. The covalent bonds between carbon atoms explain the stability of organic molecules, the formation of macromolecules and the energetic facts around specific classes of chemical reactions. Similarly with other types of bonds.

Adopting an OSR view of bonds allows to maintain both the ideal of unity and the reality of bonds. Unity is maintained because OSR – applied to the case of bonds – posits a compositional relation between bonds and their subatomic entities that is diachronic and dynamic (Ladyman 2017: 152). This understanding of dependence is consonant with accepted scientific knowledge that the interactions of electrons and nuclei (which form a bond) are dynamic: subatomic particles move around the molecule and occupy different orbitals at different times. By advocating this non-static understanding of dependence an important feature of chemical bonding is thus illuminated: bonds are diachronic and dynamic, and result from subatomic particles which interact via (mostly) Coulomb forces.

That it is a realist account follows from Dennett's understanding of patterns, as he takes that to be a pattern is to be real. This of course can be resisted; why does being a pattern automatically imply that patterns are real? While this seems to be taken by Dennett as a primitive fact about patterns, the additional requirement of OSR that real patterns figure in nomological and counterfactual generalisations offers sufficient support as to their reality. This is because, similarly to strong emergence, the realist feature of OSR is based on the acceptance of Alexander's dictum (i.e. that to be is to cause).

Admittedly, this is a very short exposition of how an account of unity can be applied to a case in chemistry and invoked to support its reality. There are many questions and problems that this (and any) account needs to address before we can convincingly argue that it should be accepted. In any case, I take the purpose of this presentation to be fulfilled. I showed that it is possible to maintain the unity of chemistry with quantum physics without holding an eliminativist stance on chemical ontology. This goes against the received view in the philosophy of chemistry and opens new avenues for research around the metaphysics of chemistry.

Finally, can the account of real patterns or any other account of (dis)unity be generalised to all chemical ontology? To answer this, it is essential to examine each chemical entity separately, including molecules, structure, orbitals and electronegativity. My suspicion is that each case relates differently to its physical constituents, or at least requires its own account of how it relates to them. This is because any account should be informed by the scientific details regarding how precisely chemistry and quantum physics each describes, explains and represents the chemical entity in question. As the case of the chemical bond illustrates, the specific details help us understand an entity's relation to its physical parts and offer empirical evidence to support a metaphysical position. Without looking at the models, representations, explanations and concepts that scientists use in order to understand and describe a chemical entity, one cannot offer an accurate metaphysical account of it.

So, before defending a specific metaphysical worldview about chemistry, we should remain neutral and examine the body of knowledge offered by the relevant sciences. It might turn out that different chemical entities relate in substantially different ways to their physical constituents: some may be reducible in a Nagelian (or other) manner, others may be patterns of physical interactions, or grounded to their physical parts. Still others may even be substantially independent of their physical constituents. From the perspective of the realist question, this implies that one may hold more than one view as to the reality of chemical stuff and its relation to physical stuff. Some chemical entities may be eliminable; others may be real because they are causally autonomous or real patterns; and still others may just be useful fictions. Identifying the ontology of chemistry is a fascinating multidimensional project.

4 Laws and Causes
Periodic Table and Chemical Reactions

The previous sections discussed metaphysical issues that have been extensively examined from the perspective of chemistry. This section is about two topics which have not received similar attention: laws of nature and causation.

Talk of causation and laws is ubiquitous in scientific discourse. Scientists talk of *causes* when explaining a phenomenon, and predict the behaviour of physical, chemical or biological systems by invoking a *law* from the relevant science. So, it is no surprise that philosophers examine what these terms designate (if anything). Among the questions asked are: does science discover laws of nature, and if so, what are their general features? Are there only fundamental physical laws or are there also special science laws? Do laws represent necessary connections or mere regularities? Similarly for causation. Are there genuine causal relations and what is their nature? Are there only physical causes or also chemical, biological and mental causes? There are also questions about the relation between causation and lawhood. For example, are laws expressions of causal relations? Do causes operate in accordance to laws of nature, and vice versa, or are both required to determine how things in the world behave?[81]

Discussion of these issues abstracts away from our everyday understanding of the world, or even from the nuanced understandings we form by studying science. However, we cannot have a complete understanding of the world without answering whether (and in what way) there are causes and laws. In the metaphysics of science, the study of physics and biology has been vital to understand laws and causation, whereas chemistry has not analogously informed these topics.[82] There are of course exceptions. For example, Hendry (2012b) posits downward causation to understand molecular structure, and Goodwin (2012) investigates chemical reactions from the perspective of mechanistic causation. The laws of thermodynamics and the ideal gas law (to the extent that they are considered part of chemical practice) have been invoked to understand laws of nature (e.g. Cartwright 1983; Needham 1991). Nevertheless, it is still the case that – despite the richness of chemistry – little has been said about laws and causation in chemistry.

Section 4 shows how laws and causation can be investigated with respect to two areas which, despite their enormous significance to chemistry and science, have not been considered from this perspective so far, namely, the periodic table and chemical reactions, respectively. This is a preliminary analysis, the aim of which is to reveal neglected interconnections between chemistry and metaphysics, and to point out questions in the metaphysics of chemistry that are worth pursuing.

4.1 Laws in Chemistry

'All noble gases are unreactive.' 'All uranium spheres are less than a mile in diameter.' 'Whenever acids react with bases they form a salt.' These universal generalisations posit some form of regularity or uniformity in nature. Statements about regularities or uniformities in nature are considered candidate expressions of laws of nature.[83]

The idea of laws has had great significance throughout the history of human thought. The term 'law' is used in diverse aspects of human life to mean different things, often being assigned prescriptive or descriptive connotations. For example, in the context of the judiciary, 'law' has prescriptive force, relating to systems of rules that communities construct and commit to obey.

---

[81] As with previous topics, those of laws and causation have a rich literature that I cannot fairly reference. So, I direct the reader to Carroll 2020.

[82] For discussions of laws in biology, e.g. Brandon 1997; Mitchell 2000.

[83] As shown in this section, not all law-like statements express laws of nature.

It has also been associated, both literally and metaphorically, with the idea of a divine rule or intention.

In the present context, the idea of lawhood that is of interest is the one invoked within the sciences to refer to regularities in nature. As Ruby states, '(a)pparently without reservation, for over three hundred years scientists have called the intelligible, measurable, predictable regularities they find in nature "laws"' (1986: 341). Under this understanding of the term, historians usually track its use to Kepler and his astronomical writings but grant primary credit to Descartes (e.g. Ott 2022). Without going into detail about the history of this idea and its role in science, it is clear that the concept is far from an obscure metaphysical invention proposed by philosophers. It has been invoked by some of the most important scientists in history to characterise some of the most profound developments in science, including by Newton in physics and Mendeleev in chemistry.

This does not mean that scientists haven't objected to using this term. For example, Boyle could not 'conceive how a body devoid of understanding and sense, truly so called, can moderate and determinate its own motions, especially so as to make them conformable to laws, that is has no knowledge or apprehension of' (quote in Ruby 1986: 341). However, the idea which Boyle rejects is one of laws as prescriptive sets of rules (Ruby 1986: 341). This is not the idea of empirically discoverable regularities later developed by Descartes and invoked by scientists to this day.

Laws of nature have interested philosophers because they relate them to the special status enjoyed by science, relative to other fields of human inquiry. On this view, science is taken to be trustworthy because it uncovers laws of nature. In fact, the discovery of laws is often taken to be the defining characteristic of science, which distinguishes it from pseudoscience (e.g. Davidson 2002; Kim 2010: 286; Ruse 1982). Several examples from science have been investigated as paradigmatic candidates of laws of nature, including Newton's law of gravity, the law of supply and demand in economics and the laws of thermodynamics.

Philosophical discussions of laws of nature revolve around the need to understand whether things in the world behave the way they do by necessity or by accident. Different answers to this have produced diverse views about laws of nature, ranging from a strong metaphysical commitment to an anti-realist stance about them. From a realist perspective, there are regularities in nature that exist mind-independently, and which enjoy – contrary to accidental regularities – lawful status (Psillos 2014: 18).[84]

---

[84] This is in line with the general spirit of scientific realism sketched in Section 3.

The latter feature is standardly spelled out in two ways: the regularity and necessitarian view of laws. According to the regularity view, laws of nature are those regularities 'that are expressed by the axioms and theorems of an ideal deductive system of our knowledge of the world, and in particular, of a deductive system that strikes the best balance between simplicity and strength' (Psillos 2014: 17; e.g. Lewis 1973; Ramsey 1978).[85] Being part of the ideal deductive system is what differentiates lawful regularities from merely accidental ones, as the latter would not be included in the best deductive system. This view is considered a modest realist account of laws in the sense that it takes that 'all there is in the world is a vast mosaic of local matters of particular fact, just one little thing and then another' (Lewis 1986: ix). This is not so with the necessitarian view, which takes laws to be necessitation relations between properties (often construed as universals) (e.g. Armstrong 1983; Dretske 1977; Tooley 1977). While there are disagreements among proponents of this view about the precise nature of necessity, it is agreed that things in the world behave as they do because they *must* behave so. Put differently, this view adds one more feature to laws of nature: 'laws tell us what (in some sense) must happen, not merely what has and will happen (given certain initial conditions)' (Dretske 1977: 263).

Regardless of how strong one's commitment to laws is, there are some commonly accepted features that help distinguish between what are taken to be legitimate candidates of laws from merely accidental regularities in nature. Distinguishing between lawful and accidental regularities is not obvious. Compare, for instance, the statements 'all gold spheres are less than a mile in diameter' and 'all uranium spheres are less than a mile in diameter'. Both have the same syntactical form and as far as we know are correct. Yet the statement about gold does not express a law of nature (van Fraassen 1989). This is because it is physically possible that a golden sphere of such a size existed. This is not so with uranium. According to our best current physics, uranium's critical mass makes it physically impossible to form spheres larger than a mile in diameter. So, we cannot admit any observed regularity as a candidate law; there are accidental regularities which – as such – should not be understood as laws (van Fraassen 1989: 27).

This section focuses on a central pillar of chemistry – the periodic table – and presents the grounds we have to believe that it represents a law. I argue that the table – if construed as expressing a law of nature – is not a representation of a single law but represents multiple regularities between various sets of

---

[85] This is also called the Mill-Ramsey-Lewis view of laws.

chemical elements.[86] That is, it is a representation of multiple laws of nature. I then discuss certain challenges that undermine this claim.

Case IX. Periodic Table

The modern periodic table is a visual representation of all known chemical elements. The elements are positioned in the table in terms of increasing atomic number. Starting with hydrogen at the top left, the elements are positioned consecutively from left to right and top to bottom. Based on this ordering, chemists distinguish between sets of elements in the table: the elements found in the same horizontal line are said to form 'groups' and the elements found in the same vertical line form 'periods'. The identification of groups and periods is useful in chemistry because members of a group or period have specific chemical or physical properties in common. This allows chemists to make inferences, predictions and explanations about chemical and physical phenomena.

Reference to a 'periodic law' emerged from the very beginning of the inquiry into the classification of chemical elements (Pulkkinen 2020). In the nineteenth century, Newlands used several times the term 'periodic law' to refer to his proposed classification of elements, and in his attempt to claim priority over Mendeleev and Meyer's classifications, stated:

> I claim to have been the first to publish a list of the elements in order of their atomic weight, and also the first to describe the periodic law, showing the existence of a simple relation between them when so arranged. (Newlands, 1884: vi–vii; Pulkkinen 2020: 182)

In 1871, Mendeleev published his paper 'Periodic Law', where he proposed 'the law of periodicity . . . that was applicable to study the relations between the properties and the atomic weights of all of the elements' (quote from Pulkkinen 2020: 196). Even though Newland's, Meyer's and Mendeleev's versions of the table have been discarded, the term 'periodic law' is still used with respect to the modern table. One need not go further than Wikipedia to find that the table is defined as 'a graphic formulation of the periodic law, which states that the properties of the chemical elements exhibit an approximate periodic dependence on their atomic numbers'.[87]

Despite the metaphysical significance of laws, philosophers have either not picked up on or undermined the periodic table's relevance to the discussion of

---

[86] To formulate this argument, I presuppose a realist stance to laws of nature, without committing to a specific view about the nature of laws (e.g. as per the regularity or necessitarian view). The goal is not to defend the reality of laws but rather to show that the periodic table is a legitimate case study to consider as such.

[87] https://en.wikipedia.org/wiki/Periodic_table.

laws (e.g. Scerri 2012, 2020). An exception is Woody (2014), who has stated (without further argument) that the periodic table could be viewed as a candidate law from the perspective of Mitchell's (2000) pragmatic account. In general, however, the periodic table has been investigated either as a theory (Hettema and Kuipers 1988; Weisberg 2007) or as a taxonomic representation (Scerri 2012, 2020; Shapere 1977).

So, how can we argue that the periodic table is a representation of a law of nature? I argue that there are several regularity relations identified by the table and which should be viewed as candidate laws. These regularity relations are much more precise than what is standardly understood as 'the periodic law' and are expressed by multiple statements that are embedded in the table. These statements include for example that 'Actinium reacts rapidly with oxygen'; 'Halogens undergo redox reactions with metal halides in solution'; and 'Lanthanum reacts with the halogens at room temperature.' That is, the periodic table is a (visual) depiction of regularities between individual elements, between sets of elements and between elements and sets of elements. The visual depiction of elements in a specific ordering, together with the posited classifications into groups and periods, allow chemists to form statements about the chemical and physical properties of different sets of elements.

So, if the periodic table represents a law of nature, it represents many laws of nature. This shouldn't come as a surprise; the table identifies 118 elements, 18 groups and 7 periods, positing various regularity relations between them about – among other things – their chemical reactivity, their (non-)metallic character, their electron affinity and ionisation energy.

Note that, I claim, the periodic table *represents* (or *identifies*) laws of nature. An equivalent way I state this is this: non-accidental regularity relations are *expressed* by statements that are embedded in the periodic table. Here, these are taken as equivalent ways for saying that there are laws in the periodic table. I do not adopt a philosophically informed understanding of 'representation' in spelling out this claim. I employ the terms only to bring forward the idea that chemists employ the periodic table as a means to visually depict and empirically examine regularity relationships between elements.

Moving on, even if we admit that there are many empirically observable regularity relations expressed within the table, we need an argument for why these regularities have lawful status. After all, apart from accidental regularities in nature (such as about the size of gold spheres mentioned previously), there are regularity relations posited by science which are not granted lawful status. As Carroll (2020) notes, 'the regularity of the ocean tides, the perihelion of Mercury's orbit, the photoelectric effect, that the universe is expanding' do not have the lawful status of – say – Newton's laws or the laws of thermodynamics.

To this end, there are certain features that are taken to be suggestive of a lawful regularity.[88] These features are generally accepted to be found in candidate laws regardless of how philosophers further understand – or disagree upon – the precise nature of laws (e.g. as per the regularity or necessitarian views). I show that they are exhibited by the regularity relations identified in the table.[89]

First, statements of laws are used to make empirically successful inferences about instances of matter (van Fraassen 1989: 29). This applies to the law-like statements of the periodic table. For example, that 'gold is unreactive' allows inferring that one's golden necklace is unreactive. Second, law-like statements allow predictions of behaviour of instances of matter in the past, present and future. Indeed, one can predict that her golden necklace will never rust based on the law that gold is unreactive.[90] Third, laws unify the behaviour of prima facie disparate things in the world. Statements about oxygen, for instance, unify how we understand the behaviour of matter, whether it is found in the sky of Athens, in a chemical laboratory in Zurich or on Mars. In turn, this implies that laws allow scientists to systematise empirical facts. Information about the chemical properties of any particular in the world (for instance of any gold substance found in jewellery, computers, mines etc.) is systematically organised by the relevant law about gold. These features are often taken to indicate that laws are universal (or statistical) claims: they hold at every time and place in the universe, and for all relevant instances of matter. Indeed, in the case of statements about (sets of) elements, these statements are taken to hold for all instances of chemical elements found anywhere and anytime in the universe (under specific conditions).

Moreover, unlike accidental generalisations, laws support counterfactual reasoning in the sense that they make counterfactual statements true (or false).[91] Indeed, this seems to be applicable to the law-like statements of the periodic table. For example, 'If a chunk of matter were made of gold, then it wouldn't rust' is made true by the periodic law that 'gold is unreactive'. Lastly, laws are taken to explain phenomena. How to spell out explanation is an issue in its own right, but it is

---

[88] Identifying these features in the law-like regularities represented by the periodic table does not suffice to argue that these regularities are laws. One needs to also spell out how these regularities are understood in terms of a metaphysical account of laws; for example in the context of the regularity or necessitarian view of laws (or some other account).

[89] Whether and which of these features are necessary and/or sufficient for establishing that a regularity is a law is debatable. I leave this open and invoke those features that standardly (though not uncontroversially) figure in the literature.

[90] What counts as a prediction – contrary to just an accommodation of known facts – has prompted debates, including with respect to the periodic table (Scerri and Worral 2001). I return to this later in this section.

[91] How to understand 'truth' is a relevant issue that needs to be further investigated.

generally agreed that laws should explain phenomena. For example, that my great-grand-mother's necklace has not corroded after 100 years is explained by the law that gold is unreactive.[92] Given the controversy over the periodic table's explanatory power, I return to this point.

Note that my view diverges from standard understandings of the 'periodic law'. Unlike Newlands, Mendeleev and modern usages of the term in both science and philosophy, I do not take 'periodic law' to refer to the existence of a periodic dependence between the properties of elements (i.e. between elements and their atomic number, as per the modern understanding of 'periodic law'). Instead, I take that there are multiple laws expressed within the table and which identify regularity relations between properties of (sets of) elements.[93]

While this is a brief analysis of the main indications of lawhood, I take this to be a good step towards believing that the law-like statements embedded in the periodic table express laws of nature. Note that this is not the first time one highlights these features of the periodic table:

> With the help of this periodic law, it is possible to organize and to systematize the chemistry of the elements into a manageable subject. Learning descriptive chemistry then becomes a process of discovery and assessment of facts, prediction and verification of chemical behavior, and evaluation of correlations and explanations. All of this leads to an understanding of why elements have the properties they do. (Mahan 1975: 569)

Interestingly, while Mahan refers to the periodic law as standardly construed (i.e. as referring to the periodic dependence of elements on their atomic number), Woody points out that it is 'implausible' that this is what he means, as this understanding of 'periodic law' is too imprecise to have the requisite explanatory and predictive power (2014: 135). I take this to reinforce my view that if we are to construe anything as the periodic law, it must be the regularity relations posited between specific properties of specific (sets of) elements.

Note that one need not be a realist about laws to admit that the regularity relations expressed in the table are legitimate candidates of laws. Consider for example the problem of ceteris paribus laws. According to Cartwright (1983), there are no laws of nature because all law-like statements in science hold ceteris paribus; that is, there are no true exceptionless regularities. Regardless of whether this criticism holds, it can be applied to the law-like statements of the table in the same way it is applied to other paradigmatic candidates of laws, such

---

[92] There are additional requirements for laws, including that statements of laws are factually – not logically – true, and that they do not involve proper names but only general concepts. I take these requirements to hold uncontroversially for the law-like statements embedded in the table.

[93] I leave open which properties should be admitted and whether they should include physical properties (such as boiling or melting point).

as Coulomb's law or Newton's laws. Take for instance the law-like statement 'Lanthanum reacts with halogens at room temperature.' This is a ceteris paribus statement because it posits a regularity relation between instances of lanthanum and halogens that only holds under specific thermodynamic conditions.[94] Of course, there are philosophers who – contrary to Cartwright – maintain that there are exceptionless law-like statements in fundamental physics which as such can be admitted as representing laws (Earman and Roberts 1999). In this context, the statements in the periodic table would be denied lawful status.[95] In any case, the fact that the law-like statements of the periodic table can figure in such discussions demonstrates that at the very least they are as good candidates as other paradigmatic candidates of laws (that are not exceptionless).

All in all, my claim is far from uncontroversial and requires a detailed exposition of its main tenets. In addition, it requires addressing issues raised by philosophers who take the table to be nothing more than a classificatory scheme (e.g. Scerri 2012, 2020). The remainder of this section briefly presents four putative problems against the periodic table representing laws.

The first problem concerns the predictive power of the periodic table. Recall that the ability to make predictions is an important feature of law-like statements. The periodic table has been lauded for its ability to not just accommodate known facts but also predict previously unknown empirical facts. Specifically, the acceptance of Mendeleev's periodic table – which is the precursor of the modern periodic table – is attributed to its ability to predict new elements, including gallium, scandium and germanium:

> When Mendeleev produced a theory of the periodic table that accounted for all sixty [really sixty-two] known elements, the scientific community was only mildly impressed. When he went on to use his theory to predict the existence of two unknown elements that were then independently detected, the Royal Society awarded him its Davy Medal ... Sixty accommodations paled next to two predictions. (Lipton 1991: 134)

However, Scerri and Worrall claim that 'the impression of consistent predictive success for Mendeleev's scheme is a complete misrepresentation of history' (2001: 419). Among other things, Mendeleev posited the existence of at least two elements that are lighter than hydrogen, as well as six new elements between hydrogen and lithium. Both predictions turned out to be false (Scerri and Worrall 2001: 420–1). Moreover, there were several unsuccessful predictions of the properties of known elements, including about the melting point of gallium and

---

[94] There are several other exceptions to the dependences posited in the table that further reinforce this.
[95] Others offer alternative ways to accommodate so-called idealisation laws (e.g. Friend 2022). This is another interesting perspective through which to examine the lawful regularities of the periodic table.

the solubility of aka-boron (2001: 422). In addition, Scerri and Worrall challenge the predictive success of Mendeleev's table on methodological grounds, arguing that 'Mendeleev ... was operating within a general and rather loose framework, underpinned by no very definite theory, and was feeling his way towards making particular predictions rather than being in possession of a theory that makes them willy nilly' (2001: 440).

On the other hand, Weisberg (2007) maintains that the successful prediction of new elements by Mendeleev is evidence that the table is not a classificatory scheme (but a theory). On his view, the methodology by which Mendeleev predicted those elements was not an exercise to fill missing gaps; it was based on hypothesising missing elements and analysing the theoretical structure Mendeleev had created via his proposed ordering of elements (Weisberg 2007: 214).

The second problem concerns the explanatory power of the periodic table. Scerri (2020) claims that the periodic table lacks genuine explanatory power because quantum physics, and in particular reference to the electronic configuration of elements, does all the explaining of the relevant phenomena. Therefore, the table is explanatorily redundant. While this worry is not addressed against what I take here to be the candidate laws of the periodic table, it is nevertheless a relevant worry as it is a standardly accepted feature of laws that they explain.

A possible reply is that we need to distinguish between what a law explains and how a law is explained. Take for instance a paradigmatic candidate law: $PV = nRT$ (the ideal gas law). Granted, the law itself does not explain why this mathematical relation holds between pressure, volume and temperature. One could even claim that statistical mechanics offers an explanation of why this relation holds between these properties. Nevertheless, one can still maintain that this law-like statement has explanatory power as it explains how particular instances of matter behave when we increase – say – their temperature. A similar response can be formulated about the regularities expressed within the table. Take for instance 'actinium reacts rapidly with oxygen'. The electronic configuration of actinium and oxygen may explain why they react the way they do. Nevertheless, this does not diminish the statement's explanatory power with respect to observed instances of chemical transformations. That is, the observed course of chemical transformation of any particular instance of actinium is explained by invoking this statement. A similar response is offered by Woody who states:

> Obviously the periodic table does not tell us why the patterns it displays exist, and a theory of atomic electronic structure may indeed help with this. . . . The issue at hand, however, is whether the table may be considered explanatory of the properties of elements and substances. What explains the patterns themselves is a separate issue, in principle, and one that raises familiar questions concerning levels of explanation and threats of regress. (2014: 137)

In fact, it is worth noting that – contrary to Scerri (2020) – Woody maintains that the periodic table is explanatory and even connects its explanatory power with its status as a law. She claims that the table identifies patterns among chemical elements, which play a vital (though not sufficient) role in the explanations invoked in chemical practice (2014: 141). Woody's idea that the table identifies patterns complements nicely how certain philosophers spell out lawful regularities in terms of real patterns (as per Dennett 1991, see Section 3; e.g. Kimpton-Nye 2022; Ladyman and Ross 2007; Psillos 2014: 23). While this is by no means a sufficient analysis, this point further reinforces the legitimacy of viewing the table as a representation of laws of nature.

However, an additional problem is prompted by considering the role of quantum physics in explaining chemical behaviour. This problem has been raised against special science laws in general, and is partly based on the adoption of a reductionist perspective towards the special sciences (e.g. Fodor 1980; Kim 2010). The worry is often formulated (though not exclusively) in terms of the overdetermination problem. According to this problem, if we accept that every non-physical event supervenes on a physical one and that – construed as an effect – the physical event always has a physical cause, then we cannot accept that this same effect also has a non-physical (say chemical) cause, because then we would have the (unacceptable) result that an effect has more than one causes. Therefore, we should reject that there is anything else than physical causes. If we further assume that explanations track causal relations (i.e. they are statements about how effects come about by causes), then we are lead to conclude that there are no special science explanations and hence no special science laws. Instead, everything is explained by physical laws.

Evidently, this issue boils down to the question of whether there are special science laws or only fundamental laws. The motivation for this scepticism against special science laws is that if special science regularities are somehow 'grounded' on more fundamental physical regularities, then perhaps we shouldn't grant to the former lawful status (e.g. Davidson 2002; Fodor 1989; Psillos 2014). As Kim states:

> [T]he phenomena investigated by the special sciences are part of the all-encompassing physical domain, how can there be special-science laws and explanations in addition to physical laws and explanations? That is, how are special sciences possible? And even if they are possible, do we need them? Why shouldn't developed physics meet all our needs? Or, to repeat Fodor, why is there anything except physics? (2010: 284)

Note that this problem involves many assumptions regarding how we should construe laws, causes, explanations and reductions. Philosophers have analysed extensively the relations between these ideas and reviewed these relations to offer different responses. While I do not present these responses here, it is evident that the postulation of laws in the periodic table hinges on how we respond to these general worries about special science laws.

One last challenge arises if we accept – as some do – that laws are regularities between natural kinds (Bird and Tobin 2022). If this is the case, one has to offer support not only for the claim that chemical elements correspond to natural kinds. One has to also support the claim that sets of elements correspond to kinds. This is because some of the law-like statements in the table concern relations between groups or periods (such as alkali metals and noble gases). And arguing that groups or periods correspond to natural kinds may not be as uncontroversial, especially if one adheres to the hierarchy requirement for natural kinds (see Section 2.2).[96] Therefore, it might turn out that not all law-like statements in the table correspond to laws of nature.

All in all, there is evidence in favour and against the claim that the regularities identified within the table are laws of nature. Whichever position one maintains, whether the periodic table represents any laws is an interesting question to raise. To answer it, we need to pursue (a) a historically informed analysis of the table; (b) a scientifically rigorous analysis, especially in terms of the table's relation to quantum physics; and (c) a careful conceptual analysis of laws and the subsequent metaphysical commitments involved.

4.2 Causation in Chemistry

Discussion of laws is almost inseparable from that of causation. From the perspective of the metaphysics of science, causation is a concept that requires domain-specific and scientifically informed analysis to clarify its content and appreciate its role in science. To this end, this final section examines how chemical reactions can be understood as expressions of causal relations and briefly presents certain unique features of reactions that inform in novel ways our understanding of causation.

Case X. Chemical Reactions

It is hard to overstate the importance of chemical reactions in understanding nature and sustaining life. From lighting fires and fermenting bread to breathing, developing life-saving drugs and creating (and tackling) climate change, there

---

[96] I would like to thank the anonymous reviewer who pointed this out.

are few activities in our everyday life that are not the result of naturally occurring or synthetic chemical reactions.

Chemical reactions refer to transformations of chemical substances that do not involve changes in the atomic number of the substances' constituting elements. I distinguish between two forms of reaction statements in chemistry. First, there are statements of reactions that occur between specific chemical substances under specified thermodynamic and environmental conditions, and which lead to the production of specific substances (henceforth called 'individual reactions'). For example, solutions of hydrochloric acid react with sodium hydroxide to produce sodium chloride and water: $HCl + NaOH \rightarrow NaCl + H_2O$.

Second, there are statements which describe chemical transformations between types of substances within a range of conditions (henceforth called 'general reactions').[97] For example, the above reaction is a special case of the acid-based reaction which occurs between an acid and a base to produce an ionic salt and water: $HA + BOH \rightarrow BA + H_2O$.

So far, philosophical and historical works on chemical reactions concern issues in chemical education: the history of chemistry; conceptual analysis; the relation of chemistry with biology; and even the metaphysics of chemistry (Harré 2008; Martins 2019; Moretti 2015; Šima 2013; Villani 2017). However, none of this work offers an account of what chemical reactions are, nor draws insight from the extensive body of knowledge on causation and laws of nature. In fact, there is little overlap of the philosophical study of chemical reactions with the literature on metaphysics of science. In part this is because the philosophy of chemistry primarily focuses on the analysis of chemical elements and substances, atoms and molecules, chemical bonds and the relation of chemistry with quantum physics. While these issues offer valuable insight on chemical reactions, an understanding of the nature of chemical reactions requires investigating them in their own right. Chemical reactions hold an ineliminable role in conveying what it is that determines the course of a chemical transformation, and this role cannot be substituted by only identifying the entities and properties of the reactants.

From the perspective of chemical reactions, it is central to examine whether reactions identify genuine causal relations, and which specific understanding of causation best applies to them. Different candidate notions of causation are available within the broad distinction between Humean and anti-Humean accounts. These include the regularity view of causation, the counterfactual account, the mechanistic account and the power-based account of causation.

---

[97] I say between 'types' of substances, and not 'kinds', because I leave open that these statements involve chemical kinds. See Section 2.

The metaphysical implications of each account affect our understanding of chemical reactions as causal relations because each specifies differently how reactants cause the formation of their products.

Investigating chemical reactions as causal relations prompts questions about reactions representing laws of nature. In philosophy, the connection of laws and causation is highly contestable. Nevertheless, an analysis of existing accounts of laws can help inform whether, in what way, and if all types of chemical reactions represent laws in nature. For example, can individual reactions be appropriate candidates of laws, if laws correspond to relations among universals (see Section 4.1)? Additionally, how should we make sense of individual reactions in the context of the ceteris paribus view of laws (e.g. Cartwright 1983)? Moreover, focusing on the unique features of chemical reactions can lead to novel insight on causation and lawhood. To demonstrate this, the remainder of this section briefly presents four such features.

First, a typical chemical reaction is *not* an event where chemical substances irreversibly transform into other substances (just like – say – a rock would irreversibly cause the shattering of a window). Instead, a reaction is a dynamic process which – once at equilibrium – results in a state where the system continuously and at a constant rate transforms into the products and reverses back into the reactants. This is a highly interesting feature of reactions when viewed from the perspective of causation. It suggests that reactions exhibit causal loops and as such they either should not be considered as genuine causal relations or they pose a challenge for those Humean and non-Humean accounts of causation that require the temporal priority of causes (e.g. Mumford and Anjum 2011).

Second, any account of causation applied to chemical reactions needs to accommodate the role of catalysts in the realisation of reactions. A catalyst is a 'substance that increases the rate of a reaction without modifying the overall standard Gibbs energy change in the reaction' (IUPAC 2014: 220). Their presence can be said to partly cause a reaction (as their absence often explains why a reaction does not take place), even though they do not substantively participate in the reaction (because they do not transform into products). This explains why chemists include them as both a reactant and a product in a chemical reaction statement. However, it raises the question of whether they should be construed as genuine causes of a reaction or as part of the environment which accommodates the reaction's realisation.

Third, chemical reactions are products of multi-level theories. The description of a chemical reaction in terms of the standard arrowed equation (i.e. $A + B \rightarrow AB$) is the result of a body of knowledge that comes from a combination of higher- and lower-level theories, most notably quantum physics and thermodynamics (e.g. Keeler and Others 2003). This makes them a unique example from the perspective of special science causation and lawhood as it raises the question of whether chemical reactions are eliminable or reducible to more fundamental causal relations and laws in physics.

Lastly, any account of causation needs to accommodate the role of reaction mechanisms in describing chemical reactions. Reaction mechanisms are descriptions of the process the reactants undergo during a chemical transformation. They specify the properties of intermediary entities and transition states formed during a reaction (IUPAC 2014: 902). The prevalence of reaction mechanisms in the explanation of chemical reactions has prompted philosophers to advocate a mechanistic view of chemical explanation (e.g. Goodwin 2012; Weininger 2014). While such a view suggests that a mechanistic account of causation is plausible for chemical reactions, this has not been explicitly examined.

So, thinking of chemical reactions from the perspective of causation can be extremely informative not only for those who wish to understand the natural of chemical reactions but also for those who are interested in forming a scientifically well-informed view of causation. Admittedly, causation is one of the most controversial ideas in metaphysics, with many philosophers dismissing it as 'a relic of a bygone age' (Russell 1912). Perhaps thinking of it from the perspective of chemical reactions will offer a novel way to understand causation that even its most persistent critics could accept.

5 Conclusion

While I have defended here my own views on chemical kinds, realism, unity and lawhood, it is not these that I wish the reader to primarily take from this Element. The main goal has been to illuminate the under-explored ideas that can be revealed by practicing metaphysics from a chemical perspective. Despite what one might believe, even those metaphysical issues which have been extensively discussed with respect to chemistry are far from settled. Whether chemical elements and compounds correspond to natural kinds is, for example, a question that can hold unexpected answers if we look further into the scientific details that pertain to the analysis of those entities. Similarly, chemistry's reduction to quantum physics and how it informs our views on the reality of chemical stuff remains an open issue which can be informed by investigating modern accounts from the general philosophical literature. Moreover, there are issues within metaphysics that have been largely neglected in the philosophy of chemistry, even though there are chemical case studies that can inform them in truly novel ways. Chemical reactions as causal relations and the periodic table as a candidate law of nature are such examples.

Evidently, there are more questions in metaphysics that can be similarly informed by chemistry. These include issues on the identity of chemical entities, on persistence during chemical change and on the nature of chemical properties. There are also additional chemical case studies which warrant philosophical analysis. For example, models in quantum chemistry which do not apply the BO approximation have been largely overlooked in the reductionist debate about chemistry. All this is unchartered territory that stands as an opportunity for novel and exciting research. My wish is that this Element encourages such pursuits within the realms of chemistry's metaphysics!

References

Achinstein, P. (2001). *The Book of Evidence*. New York: Oxford University Press.

Aristotle. (1999). *Metaphysics*, J. Sachs (trans.). New Mexico: Green Lion Press.

Armstrong, D. M. (1983). *What Is a Law of Nature?* Cambridge: Cambridge University Press.

Austin, J. L. (1962). *How to Do Things with Words*. Oxford: Clarendon Press.

Ball, P. (2021). *The Elements: A Visual History of Their Discovery*. Chicago: The University Chicago Press.

Bartol, J. (2016). Biochemical kinds. *British Journal for the Philosophy of Science, 67*, 531–51.

Bartoš, H., & King, C. (eds.). (2020). *Heat, Pneuma, and Soul in Ancient Philosophy and Science*. Cambridge: Cambridge University Press.

Bellazzi, F. (2022). Biochemical functions. *British Journal for the Philosophy of Science*. https://doi.org/10.1086/723241.

Bird, A. (2018). The metaphysics of natural kinds. *Synthese, 195*(4), 1397–426.

Bird, A., & Tobin, E. (2022). Natural kinds. *The Stanford Encyclopedia of Philosophy*, E. N. Zalta (ed.) (Spring 2022 ed.). https://plato.stanford.edu/archives/spr2022/entries/natural-kinds/.

Blumenthal, G., & Ladyman, J. (2017). The development of problems within the phlogiston theories, 1766–1791. *Foundations of Chemistry, 19*(3), 241–80.

Blumenthal, G., & Ladyman, J. (2018). Theory comparison and choice in chemistry, 1766–1791. *Foundations of Chemistry, 20*, 169–89.

Boyd, R. N. (1983). On the current status of the issue of scientific realism. *Erkenntnis, 19*(1/3), 45–90. https://doi.org/10.1007/BF00174775.

Boyle, R. (2003). *The Sceptical Chemist: The Classic 1661 Text*. Mineola, NY: Dover Publications, Inc..

Brading, K. (2010). Autonomous patterns and scientific realism. *Philosophy of Science, 77*(5), 827–39.

Brandon, R. N. (1997). Does biology have laws? The experimental evidence. *Philosophy of Science, 2*, 444–57.

Brock, W. (2012). *The Fontana History of Chemistry*. London: HarperCollins UK.

Brown, R. G., & Ladyman, J. (2019). *Materialism: A Historical and Philosophical Inquiry*. London: Routledge.

Bursten, J. R. (2014). Microstructure without essentialism: A new perspective on chemical classification. *Philosophy of Science, 81*(4), 633–53.

Bursten, J. R. (2016). Smaller than a Breadbox: Scale and natural kinds. *The British Journal for the Philosophy of Science, 69*(1), 1–23.

Carnap, R. (1928/1967). *The Logical Structure of the World and Pseudoproblems in Philosophy*. Berkeley: University of California Press.

Carroll, J. W. (2020). Laws of nature. *The Stanford Encyclopedia of Philosophy*, E. N. Zalta (ed.). https://plato.stanford.edu/archives/win2020/entries/laws-of-nature/.

Cartwright, N. (1983). *How the Laws of Physics Lie*. Oxford: Oxford University Press.

Cat, J. (2022). The unity of science. *The Stanford Encyclopedia of Philosophy*, E. N. Zalta (ed.). https://plato.stanford.edu/archives/spr2022/entries/scientific-unity/.

Chakravartty, A. (2007). *A Metaphysics for Scientific Realism: Knowing the Unobservable*. Cambridge, UK: Cambridge University Press.

Chalmers, A. (2011). Drawing philosophical lessons from Perrin's experiments on Brownian motion: A response to van Fraassen. *British Journal for the Philosophy of Science*, *62*, 711–32.

Chang, H. (2012a). Acidity: The persistence of the everyday in the scientific. *Philosophy of Science*, *79*(5), 690–700.

Chang, H. (2012b). *Is Water H2O? Evidence, Realism and Pluralism* (Vol. 293). Springer Dordrecht: Science & Business Media.

Chang, H. (2015a). Reductionism and the relation between chemistry and physics. In T. Arabatzis, Renn, J., & Simões, A. (ed.), *Relocating the History of Science*. Boston Studies in the Philosophy and History of Science (Vol. 312) (pp. 193–209). Dordrecht: Springer.

Chang, H. (2015b). The rising of chemical natural kinds through epistemic iteration. In Catherine Kendig (ed.), *Natural Kinds and Classification in Scientific Practice* (pp. 33–46). London: Routledge.

Chang, H. (2016). Pragmatic realism. *Journal of Humanities of Valparaiso*, (8), 107–22.

Cláudio, M. N., Roque, J. P. L., Doddipatla, S., et al. (2022). Simultaneous tunneling control in conformer-specific reactions. *Journal of the American Chemical Society*, *144*(45), 20866–74. https://doi.org/10.1021/jacs.2c09026.

Coulson, C. A. (1955). The contributions of wave mechanics to chemistry. *Journal of the Chemical Society (Resumed)*, 2069–84. https://pubs.rsc.org/en/content/articlelanding/1955/jr/jr9550002069/unauth

Darden, L., & Maull, N. (1977). Interfield theories. *Philosophy of Science*, *44*(1), 43–64. www.jstor.org/stable/187099.

Davidson, D. (2002). Mental events. In Paul K. Moser, & J. D. Trout (eds.), *Contemporary Materialism* (pp. 122–37). London: Routledge.

Dennett, D. C. (1991). Real patterns. *The Journal of Philosophy*, *88*(1), 27–51.

Dirac, P. (1929). The quantum mechanics of many-electron systems. *Proceedings of the Royal Society of London*, Series A, Containing Papers of a Mathematical and Physical Character, *123*(792), 714–33.

Dretske, F. (1977). Referring to events. In P. French, T. Uehling Jr. & H. Wettstein (eds.), *Midwest Studies in Philosophy II* (pp. 90–9). Minneapolis: University of Minnesota Press.

Duhem, P. ([1914] 1991). *The Aim and Structure of Physical Theory* (Vol. 13). New Jersey: Princeton University Press.

Dupré, J. (1993). *The Disorder of Things: Metaphysical Foundations of the Disunity of Science*. Cambridge, MA: Harvard University Press.

Earman, J., & Roberts, J. (1999). Ceteris paribus, there is no problem of provisos. *Synthese*, *118*, 439–78.

Ellis, B. (2001). *Scientific Essentialism*. Cambridge Studies in Philosophy. Cambridge: Cambridge University Press.

Ellis, B. (2002). *The Philosophy of Nature: A Guide to the New Essentialism*. London: Routledge.

Fine, A. (1986). Unnatural attitudes: Realist and antirealist attachments to science. *Mind*, *95*(378), 149–77. https://doi.org/10.1093/mind/XCV.378.149.

Fine, K. (1994). Essence and modality. In J. E. Tomberlin (ed.), *Philosophical Perspectives 8: Logic and Language* (pp. 1–16). Atascadero: Ridgeview.

Fodor, J. A. (1980). Special Sciences, or the Disunity of Science as a Working Hypothesis. In B. Ned (ed.), *Readings in Philosophy of Psychology, Volume I* (pp. 120–33). Cambridge, MA: Harvard University Press.

Fodor, J. A. (1985). Fodor's guide to mental representation: The intelligent auntie's vade-mecum. *Mind*, *94*(373), 76–100.

Fodor, J. A. (1989). Making mind matter more. *Philosophical Topics*, *17*, 59–79.

Franklin, A., & Seifert, V. A. (2020). The problem of molecular structure just is the measurement problem. *The British Journal for the Philosophy of Science*, 1–38. https://doi.org/10.1086/715148.

Franklin-Hall, L. R. (2015). Natural kinds as categorical bottlenecks. *Philosophical Studies*, *172*, 925–48.

French, S. (2014). *The Structure of the World: Metaphysics and Representation*. Oxford: Oxford University Press.

Friend, T. (2019). Can parts cause their wholes? *Synthese*, *196*, 5061–82.

Friend, T. T. (2022). How to be Humean about idealisation laws. *Philosophy of Science*, (2023), *90*, 150–170. https://doi.org/10.1017/psa.2022.12.

Frigg, R., & Votsis, I. (2011). Everything you always wanted to know about structural realism but were afraid to ask. *European Journal for Philosophy of Science*, *1*, 227–76.

Gavroglu, K., & Simões, A. (2011). *Neither Physics nor Chemistry: A History of Quantum Chemistry*. Cambridge, MA: MIT Press.

Goodwin, W. (2011). Structure, function, and protein taxonomy. *Biology & Philosophy, 26*(4), 533–45.

Goodwin, W. (2012). Mechanisms and chemical reactions. In R. Hendry, P. Needham & A. Woody (eds.), *Handbook of the Philosophy of Science, Vol. 6: Philosophy of Chemistry* (pp. 301–27). Amsterdam: Elsevier.

Häggqvist, S. (2022). No, water (still) doesn't have a microstructural essence (reply to Hoefer & Martí). *European Journal for Philosophy of Science, 12*(2), 1–13.

Harré, R. (2005). Chemical kinds and essences revisited. *Foundations of Chemistry, 7*(1), 7–30.

Harré, R. (2008). Some presuppositions in the metaphysics of chemical reactions. *Foundations of Chemistry, 10*, 19–38. https://doi.org/10.1007/s10698-005-9000-8.

Havstad, J. C. (2018). Messy chemical kinds. *The British Journal for the Philosophy of Science, 69*(3), 719–43.

Hawley, K., & Bird, A. (2011). What are natural kinds? *Philosophical Perspectives, 25*, 205–21.

Heitler, W., & London, F. (1927). Wechselwirkung neutraler Atome und homöopolare Bindung nach der Quantenmechanik. *Zeitschrift für Physik, 44*(6), 455–72.

Hempel, C. (1966). *Philosophy of Natural Science*. Englewood Cliffs: Prentice Hall.

Hendry, R. F. (2004). The physicists, the chemists, and the pragmatics of explanation. *Philosophy of Science, 71*(5), 1048–59.

Hendry, R. F. (2005). Lavoisier and Mendeleev on the elements. *Foundations of Chemistry, 7*(1), 31–48.

Hendry, R. F. (2006a). Elements, compounds, and other chemical kinds. *Philosophy of Science, 73*(5), 864–75.

Hendry, R. F. (2006b). Substantial confusion. *Studies in History and Philosophy of Science Part A, 37*(2), 322–36.

Hendry, R. F. (2008). Two conceptions of the chemical bond. *Philosophy of Science, 75*(5), 909–20.

Hendry, R. F. (2010). Ontological reduction and molecular structure. *Studies in History and Philosophy of Science Part B, 41*(2), 183–91.

Hendry, R. F. (2012a). Chemical substances and the limits of pluralism. *Foundations of Chemistry, 14*(1), 55–68.

Hendry, R. F. (2012b). Reduction, emergence and physicalism. In A. Woody & R. Hendry (eds.), *Philosophy of Chemistry* (pp. 367–86). Amsterdam: Elsevier.

Hendry, R. F. (2017). Prospects for strong emergence in chemistry. In F. Orilia, M. P. Paoletti (eds.), *Philosophical and Scientific Perspectives on Downward Causation* (pp. 146–63). London: Routledge.

Hendry, R. F. (2018). Scientific realism and the history of chemistry. *Spontaneous Generations: A Journal for the History and Philosophy of Science*, 9(1), 108–17.

Hettema, H. (2017). *The Union of Chemistry and Physics*. Cham: Springer International.

Hettema, H., & Kuipers, T. A. (1988). The periodic table: Its formalization, status, and relation to atomic theory. *Erkenntnis*, 28(3), 387–408.

Hoefer, C., & Martí, G. (2019). Water has a microstructural essence after all. *European Journal for Philosophy of Science*, 9(1), 1–15.

Hofmann, J. R. (1990). How the models of chemistry vie. *PSA: Proceedings of the Biennial Meeting of the Philosophy of Science Association*, 1990(1), 405–19.

Hudson, R. (2020). The reality of Jean Perrin's atoms and molecules. *The British Journal for the Philosophy of Science*, 71(1), 33–58.

Hull, D. L. (1978). A matter of individuality. *Philosophy of Science*, 45(3), 335–60.

IUPAC. (2014). *Compendium of Chemical Terminology: Gold Book*. Version 2.3.3. https://goldbook.iupac.org/pdf/goldbook.pdf (accessed 3/5/2018).

Keeler, J., & Wothers, P. (2003). *Why Chemical Reactions Happen*. Oxford: Oxford University Press.

Kemeny, J. G., & Oppenheim, P. (1956). On reduction. *Philosophical Studies: An International Journal for Philosophy in the Analytic Tradition*, 7(1/2), 6–19.

Khalidi, M. A. (1998). Natural kinds and crosscutting categories. *Journal of Philosophy*, 95(1), 33–50.

Kim, J. (1999). Making sense of emergence. *Philosophical Studies: An International Journal for Philosophy in the Analytic Tradition*, 95(1/2), 3–36.

Kim, J. (2007). *Physicalism, or Something Near Enough*. Princeton: Princeton University Press.

Kim, J. (2010). Why there are no laws in the special sciences: Three arguments. *Essays in the Metaphysics of Mind*, 282–310. Oxford: Oxford University Press

Kimpton-Nye, S. (2022). Laws of nature: Necessary and contingent. *The Philosophical Quarterly*, 72(4), 875–95.

Kincaid, H. (1997). *Individualism and the Unity of Science: Essays on Reduction, Explanation, and the Special Sciences*. Maryland: Rowman & Littlefield.

Kitcher, P. (1993). *The Advancement of Science*. New York: Oxford University Press.

Kripke, S. A. (1972). Naming and necessity. In Davidson, D., & Harman, G. (eds), *Semantics of Natural Language* (pp. 253–355). Dordrecht: Springer.

Kumaki, J. (2016). Observation of polymer chain structures in two-dimensional films by atomic force microscopy. *Polymer Journal, 48*, 3–14. https://doi.org/10.1038/pj.2015.67.

Ladyman, J. (2011). Structural realism versus standard scientific realism: The case of phlogiston and dephlogisticated air. *Synthese, 180*(2), 87–101.

Ladyman, J. (2012). *Understanding Philosophy of Science*. London: Routledge.

Ladyman, J., Slater, M., & Yudell, Z. (2017). An apology for naturalized metaphysics. In *Metaphysics and the Philosophy of Science: New Essays* (pp. 141–61). Oxford: Oxford University Press.

Ladyman, J., Ross, D., & Spurrett, D. with Collier, J. (2007). *Every Thing Must Go: Metaphysics Naturalized*. Oxford: Oxford University Press.

LaPorte, J. (1996). Chemical kind term reference and the discovery of essence. *Nous, 30*(1), 112–32.

Laudan, L. (1981). A confutation of convergent realism. *Philosophy of Science, 48*(1), 19–49.

Laudan, L. (1984). Realism without the real. *Philosophy of Science, 51*(1), 156–62.

Le Poidevin, R. (2005). Missing elements and missing premises: A combinatorial argument for the ontological reduction of chemistry. *British Journal for the Philosophy of Science, 56*(1), 117–34.

Lewis, D. (1973). *Counterfactuals*. Cambridge: Harvard University Press.

Lewis, D. (1986). *On the Plurality of Worlds* (Vol. 322). Oxford: Blackwell.

Lewis, G. N. ([1923] 1966). *Valence and the Structure of Atoms and Molecules*. New York: Dover, Chemical Catalogue.

Lipton, P. (1991). *Inference to the Best Explanation*. London: Routledge.

Locke, J. ([1689] 1975). *An Essay Concerning Human Understanding*, P. H. Nidditch (ed.). Oxford: Clarendon Press.

Lombardi, O., & Labarca, M. (2005). The ontological autonomy of the chemical world. *Foundations of Chemistry, 7*(2), 125–48.

Longy, F. (2018). Do we need two notions of natural kind to account for the history of 'jade'? *Synthese, 195*(4), 1459–86.

Lowe, E. J. (1998). *The Possibility of Metaphysics: Substance, Identity, and Time*. New York: Oxford University Press.

Lowe, E. J. (2006). *The Four-Category Ontology: A Metaphysical Foundation for Natural Science*. Oxford: Oxford University Press.

Macedo, K. G., & Haiduke, R. L. (2020). A quantum theory atoms in molecules study about the inductive effect of substituents in methane derivatives. *ACS Omega, 5*(15), 9041–5.

Magnus, P. D. (2018). Taxonomy, ontology, and natural kinds. *Synthese, 195,* 1427–39.

Mahan, B. H. (1975). *University Chemistry.* Reading: Addison-Wesley.

Martins, R. D. (2019). Émile Meyerson and mass conservation in chemical reactions: A priori expectations versus experimental tests. *Foundations of Chemistry, 21,* 109–24.

Matta, C. F. (2013). Philosophical aspects and implications of the quantum theory of atoms in molecules (QTAIM). *Foundations of Chemistry, 15,* 245–51.

Maudlin, T. (1995). Three measurement problems. *Topoi, 14*(1), 7–15.

McFarland, A. (2018). Causal powers and isomeric chemical kinds. *Synthese, 195,* 1441–57. https://doi.org/10.1007/s11229-016-1044-x.

Mill, J. S. (1884). *A System of Logic.* London: Longman.

Mitchell, S. D. (2000). Dimensions of scientific law. *Philosophy of Science, 67,* 242–65.

Moretti, G. (2015). The 'extent of reaction': A powerful concept to study chemical transformations at the first-year general chemistry courses. *Foundations of Chemistry, 17,* 107–15.

Mumford, S., & Anjum, R. L. (2011). *Getting Causes from Powers.* Oxford: Oxford University Press.

Nagel, E. (1979). *The Structure of Science: Problems in the Logic of Scientific Explanation,* 3rd ed. Indianapolis: Hackett.

Needham, P. (1991). Duhem and Cartwright on the truth of laws. *Synthese, 89* (1), 89–109.

Needham, P. (2000). What is water? *Analysis, 60*(1), 13–21.

Needham, P. (2004). When did atoms begin to do any explanatory work in chemistry? *International Studies in the Philosophy of Science, 18*(2–3), 199–219.

Needham, P. (2010). Nagel's analysis of reduction: Comments in defense as well as critique. *Studies in History and Philosophy of Science Part B, 41*(2), 163–70.

Needham, P. (2011). Microessentialism: What is the argument? *Noûs, 45*(1), 1–21.

Newlands, J. A. (1884). *On the Discovery of the Periodic Law: And on Relations among the Atomic Weights.* London: E. & F. N. Spon.

Nye, M. J. (1972). *Molecular Reality: A Perspective on the Scientific Work of Jean Perrin.* London: Macdonald.

Oppenheim, P., & Putnam, H. (1958). Unity of science as a working hypothesis. In H. Feigl, M. Scriven & G. Maxwell (ed.), *Minnesota Studies in the Philosophy of Science* (Vol. 2) (pp. 3–36). Minneapolis: University of Minnesota Press.

Ott, W. (2022). *The Metaphysics of Laws of Nature: The Rules of the Game.* Oxford: Oxford University Press.

Papineau, D. (2002). *Thinking about Consciousness.* Oxford: Clarendon Press.

Perrin, J. (1916). *Atoms.* New York: D. Van Nostrand.

Plato. (1952). *Phaedrus.* Cambridge: Cambridge University Press.

Psillos, S. (2005). *Scientific Realism: How Science Tracks Truth.* London: Routledge.

Psillos, S. (2011). Moving molecules above the scientific horizon: On Perrin's case for realism. *Journal for General Philosophy of Science, 42*, 339–63.

Psillos, S. (2014). Regularities, natural patterns and laws of nature. *Theoria: Revista de Teoría, Historia y Fundamentos de la Ciencia, 29*(1), 9–27.

Pulkkinen, K. (2020). Values in the development of early periodic tables. *Ambix, 67*(2), 174–98. https://doi.org/10.1080/00026980.2020.1747325.

Pullman, B. (2001). *The Atom in the History of Human Thought.* Oxford: Oxford University Press.

Putnam, H. (1975). *Philosophical Papers: Mathematics, Matter, and Method* (Vol. 1). Cambridge: Cambridge University Press Archive.

Quine, W. V. (1969). *Ontological Relativity and Other Essays.* New York: Columbia University Press.

Ramsey, F. (1978). *Foundations.* London: Routledge and Kegan Paul.

Reichenbach, H. (1956). *The Direction of Time.* Berkeley: University of California Press.

Ross, D. (2000). Rainforest realism: A Dennettian theory of existence. In D. Ross, A. Brook, &D. L. Thompson (eds.), *Dennett's Philosophy: A Comprehensive Assessment* (pp. 147–68). Cambridge, MA: The MIT Press.

Roush, S. (2005). *Tracking Truth: Knowledge, Evidence, and Science.* Oxford: Clarendon Press.

Ruby, J. E. (1986). The origins of scientific 'Law'. *Journal of the History of Ideas, 47*(3), 341–59.

Ruse, M. (1982). Creation science is not science. *Science, Technology, & Human Values, 7*(3), 72–8.

Russell, B. (1912). On the notion of cause. *Proceedings of the Aristotelian Society, 13*, 1–26.

Salmon, W. C. (1985). Empiricism: The Key Question. In N. Rescher (ed.), N. Rescher (ed.), *The Heritage of Logical Positivism* (pp. 1–22). Lanham: University Press of America.

Scerri, E. (1994). Has chemistry been at least approximately reduced to quantum mechanics? *PSA: Proceedings of the Biennial Meeting of the Philosophy of Science Association, 1994*, 160–70.

Scerri, E. R. (1998). Popper's naturalized approach to the reduction of chemistry. *International Studies in the Philosophy of Science, 12*(1), 33–44.

Scerri, E. R. (2012). A critique of Weisberg's view on the periodic table and some speculations on the nature of classifications. *Foundations of Chemistry, 14*(3), 275–84.

Scerri, E. R. (2020). The periodic table and the turn to practice. *Studies in History and Philosophy of Science Part A, 79*, 87–93.

Scerri, E. R. (2022). Hasok Chang on the nature of acids. *Foundations of Chemistry, 24*, 389–404. https://doi.org/10.1007/s10698-022-09432-z.

Scerri, E. R., & Fisher, G. A. (eds.). (2016). *Essays in the Philosophy of Chemistry*. Oxford: Oxford University Press.

Scerri, E. R., & Worrall, J. (2001). Prediction and the periodic table. *Studies in History and Philosophy of Science Part A, 32*(3), 407–52.

Seifert, V. A. (2017). An alternative approach to unifying chemistry with quantum mechanics. *Foundations of Chemistry, 19*, 209–22.

Seifert, V. A. (2020). The strong emergence of molecular structure. *European Journal for Philosophy of Science, 10*(3), 1–25.

Seifert, V. A. (2022a). Do molecules have structure in isolation? How models can provide the answer. In Lombardi, O., González, J. C. M., & Fortin, S. (eds.), *Philosophical Perspectives in Quantum Chemistry* (pp. 125–43). Cham: Springer.

Seifert, V. A. (2022b). The chemical bond is a real pattern. *Philosophy of Science, 90*(2), 269–87. https://doi.org/10.1017/psa.2022.17.

Shapere, D. (1977). Scientific theories and their domains. In F. Suppe (ed.), *The Structure of Scientific Theories* (pp. 518–99). Urbana: Illinois University Press.

Šima, J. (2013). Redox reactions: Inconsistencies in their description. *Foundations of Chemistry, 15*, 57–64.

Slater, M. H. (2009). Macromolecular pluralism. *Philosophy of Science, 76*(5), 851–63.

Sober, E. (2015). *Ockham's Razors: A User's Manual*. Cambridge: Cambridge University Press. https://doi.org/10.1017/CBO9781107705937.

Song, X., Yin, K., Wang, Y., et al. (2019). Exotic hydrogen bonding in compressed ammonia hydrides. *The Journal of Physical Chemistry Letters, 10* (11), 2761–6.

Stanford, P. K. (2006). *Exceeding Our Grasp: Science, History, and the Problem of Unconceived Alternatives* (Vol. 1). Oxford: Oxford University Press.

Stanford, P. K. (2009). Scientific realism, the atomic theory, and the catch-all hypothesis: Can we test fundamental theories against all serious alternatives? *The British Journal for the Philosophy of Science*, *60*(2), 253–69.

Stoljar, D. (2022). Physicalism. *The Stanford Encyclopedia of Philosophy*, E. N. Zalta (ed.). https://plato.stanford.edu/archives/sum2022/entries/physicalism/.

Tahko, T. E. (2015). Natural kind essentialism revisited. *Mind*, *124*(495), 795–822.

Tahko, T. E. (2018). The epistemology of essence. In A. Carruth, S. Gibb & J. Heil (eds.), *Ontology, Modality, and Mind: Themes from the Metaphysics of E. J. Lowe* (93–110). Oxford: Oxford University Press.

Tahko, T. E. (2020). Where do you get your protein? Or: Biochemical realization. *The British Journal for the Philosophy of Science*, *71*(3), 799–825.

Tahko, T. E. (2021). *Unity of Science*. Cambridge: Cambridge University Press.

Tahko, T. E. (2022). Natural kinds, mind-independence, and unification principles. *Synthese*, *200*, 144, 1–23. https://doi.org/10.1007/s11229-022-03661-7.

Tobin, E. (2010a). Crosscutting natural kinds and the hierarchy thesis. In H. Beebee & N. Sabbarton-Leary (eds.), *The Semantics and Metaphysics of Natural Kinds* (pp. 1–179). New York: Routledge.

Tobin, E. (2010b). Microstructuralism and macromolecules: The case of moonlighting proteins. *Foundations of Chemistry*, *12*, 41–54. https://doi.org/10.1007/s10698-009-9078-5.

Tobin, E. (2013). Are natural kinds and natural properties distinct? In S. Mumford & M. Tugby (eds.), *Metaphysics and Science* (pp. 164–82). Oxford: Oxford University Press.

Tooley, M. (1977). The nature of laws. *Canadian Journal of Philosophy*, *7*, 667–98.

Van Brakel, J. (1986). The chemistry of substances and the philosophy of mass terms. *Synthese*, *69*(3), 291–324.

Van Brakel, J. (2000). *Philosophy of Chemistry*. Leuven: Leuven University Press.

van Fraassen, B. C. (1980). *The Scientific Image*. Oxford: Oxford University Press.

Van Fraassen, B. C. (1989). *Laws and Symmetry*. Oxford: Clarendon Press.

Van Fraassen, B. C. (2009). The perils of Perrin, in the hands of philosophers. *Philosophical Studies*, *143*(1), 5–24.

van Riel, R., & Van Gulick, R. (2019). Scientific reduction. *The Stanford Encyclopedia of Philosophy*, E. N. Zalta (ed.). https://plato.stanford.edu/archives/spr2019/entries/scientific-reduction/.

Villani, G. (2017). Chemical perspective in the study of living beings: A systemic complexity approach. *Foundations of Chemistry*, *19*, 77–91.

Weininger, S. J. (2014). Reactivity and its Contexts. In U. Klein & C. Reinhardt (eds.), *Objects of Chemical Inquiry* (pp. 203–39). Leiden: Brill.

Weisberg, M. (2006). Water is not H_2O. In Baird, D., Scerri, E., & McIntyre, L. (eds.), *Philosophy of Chemistry* (pp. 337–45). Dordrecht: Springer.

Weisberg, M. (2007). Who is a modeler? *The British Journal for the Philosophy of Science*, *58*(2), 207–33.

Weisberg, M. (2008). Challenges to the structural conception of chemical bonding. *Philosophy of Science*, *75*(5), 932–46.

Whewell, W. (1860). *On the Philosophy of Discovery: Chapters Historical and Critical*. London: J. W. Parker.

Wilson, J. (2016). Metaphysical emergence: Weak and strong. In Bigaj, T., & Wüthrich, C. (eds.), *Metaphysics in Contemporary Physics*, (24 November 2015), *251*, 306–402. Leiden: Brill.

Woody, A. I. (2014). Chemistry's periodic law: Rethinking representation and explanation after the turn to practice. In L. Soler, S. Zwart, M. Lynch & V. Israel-Jost (eds.), *Science after the Practice Turn in Philosophy, History, and the Social Studies of Science* (pp. 123–50). London: Routledge Taylor & Francis Group.

Woolley, R. G. (1976). Quantum theory and molecular structure. *Advances in Physics*, *25*(1), 27–52.

Woolley, R. G., & Sutcliffe, B. T. (1977). Molecular structure and the born: Oppenheimer approximation. *Chemical Physics Letters*, *45*(2), 393–8.

Zhao, L., Pan, S., Holzmann, N., Schwerdtfeger, P., & Frenking, G. (2019). Chemical bonding and bonding models of main-group compounds. *Chemical Reviews*, *119*(14), 8781–845.

Acknowledgements

I am indebted to two anonymous referees for this Element and to James Ladyman, Tuomas Tahko, Francesca Bellazzi, Alexander Franklin, Toby Friend, Sam Kimpton-Nye, Ana-Maria Crețu, Alkistis Elliott-Graves and Nick Norman. I would also like to thank my colleagues at the University of Athens: Stathis Psillos, Maria Panagiotatou, Theodore Arabatzis, Vassilis Sakellariou, Stavros Ioannidis, Vassilis Livanios, Stelios Kampouridis and Antonis Antoniou. The research for this Element was funded by the European Research Council (ERC) under the European Union's (EU) Horizon 2020 research and innovation programme, grant agreement No 771509 ('MetaScience'), and by the Hellenic Foundation for Research & Innovation (H.F.R.I.) under the project 'NoMoS: Laws and Powers in the Metaphysics of Science'.

Cambridge Elements ᐓ

Metaphysics

Tuomas E. Tahko
University of Bristol

Tuomas E. Tahko is Professor of Metaphysics of Science at the University of Bristol, UK. Tahko specializes in contemporary analytic metaphysics, with an emphasis on methodological and epistemic issues: 'meta-metaphysics'. He also works at the interface of metaphysics and philosophy of science: 'metaphysics of science'. Tahko is the author of *Unity of Science* (Cambridge University Press, 2021, *Elements in Philosophy of Science*), *An Introduction to Metametaphysics* (Cambridge University Press, 2015) and editor of *Contemporary Aristotelian Metaphysics* (Cambridge University Press, 2012).

About the Series
This highly accessible series of Elements provides brief but comprehensive introductions to the most central topics in metaphysics. Many of the Elements also go into considerable depth, so the series will appeal to both students and academics. Some Elements bridge the gaps between metaphysics, philosophy of science, and epistemology.

Cambridge Elements ≡

Metaphysics

Printed in the USA
CPSIA information can be obtained
at www.ICGtesting.com
LVHW011256100124
768612LV00006B/326